QUEST

THE SEARCH FOR MEANING THROUGH CHRIST

QUEST

THE SEARCH FOR MEANING THROUGH CHRIST

Diogenes Allen

Walker and Company
New York, New York

First published in the United States of America in 1990
by Walker Publishing Company, Inc.

Published simultaneously in Canada by Thomas Allen & Sons
Canada, Limited, Markham, Ontario

Library of Congress Cataloging-in-Publication Data
Allen, Diogenes.
Quest: The Search For Meaning Through Christ /
Diogenes Allen.
Includes bibliographical references.
ISBN 0-8027-1101-4
1. Jesus Christ — Person and offices. 2. Bible. N.T. Gospels—
Criticism, interpretation, etc. 3. Apologetics— 20th Century.
4. Christianity — Philosophy. I Title.
BT202.A625 1990   89-48205
232 — dc20
CIP
Printed in the United States of America

2 4 6 8 10 9 7 5 3 1

For
Ray and Phyllis Lindquist
Pavilion, New York

Acknowledgment

This book was written while I was a Fellow of the Center of Theological Inquiry, Princeton, New Jersey.

I am grateful to Martinus C. de Boer for reading the Introduction and Chapter One and to Jane M. Allen and Timothy G. Allen for reading the entire manuscript and for their stylistic and substantive suggestions. I am of course wholly responsible for its inadequacies.

I have used inclusive language whenever referring to human beings. But in the case of deity I have retained the useage of the biblical translations that I have employed.

Scriptural quotations marked NEB are from the *New English Bible: New Testament*, Oxford University Press and Cambridge University Press, fourth printing, 1961. Otherwise they are from the *Revised Standard Version* of the Holy Bible, copyright © 1946, 1952, and 1971, 1973, by the Division of Christian Education, National Council of Churches of Christ in the U.S.A. and used by permission.

CONTENTS

Introduction	Light On Big Questions	xi
Chapter One	A Monstrous Mistake	1
Chapter Two	Finding Our Place	15
Chapter Three	The Teachings of Jesus	34
Chapter Four	A New Kind of Death	52
Chapter Five	Transfiguration	78
Chapter Six	Pathways to God	99

Light On Big Questions

Immanuel Kant, perhaps the greatest philosopher of modern times, summarized the big questions of life as: What can we *know*? What must we *do*? What can we *hope* for? The answers change from time to time. A civilization swings from optimistic confidence to deep despair as it goes through the ups and downs of economic prosperity and depression, wars, and natural disasters. But the big picture of the meaning and significance of life is anchored to our knowledge of science, and to the insights of philosophy, religion, and the arts.

For some time the big picture of our civilization has been viewed on a split-screen. There is a split between the heart and the head, a split that affects every one of us, whether we are religious or not.

Consider, for example, an editorial by Edwin Yoder, a syndicated columnist, that appeared in the Washington *Post* during a Christmas season. It was not the usual dressing down about the commercialization of Christmas.

Rather, it was a heartfelt description of the lost sense of wonder, which most of us perhaps regain only at Christmas time. Christmas, he wrote,

> compels us briefly to recall that minds no less sophisticated and subtle than ours . . . once gazed on the same world and saw it thick-laced with the miraculous. It did not seem at all incredible that the divine might come down to earth in the disarming disguise of a child; nor that a baby born obscurely in a small tribal society, a minor tributary of Rome, really could be the Messiah, the long-awaited redeemer.

> Such capacities to see and believe [began to] vanish some time in the seventeeth century, when the scientific revolution began to shower mankind with new miracles, of another sort, at the expense of the old way of looking at the world.

Although our world has broken in half, the writer continues,

> the quest for the special star continues. The things it symbolizes may be harder to find or to authenticate when found. But the appeal of "peace on earth", the power of redeeming innocence, still sway our small world. We long to put the two halves back together for a moment: to see a confusing and contradictory world with the singleness of wisemen and shepherds.[1]

But how do we put our world together again? Yoder exaggerates how easy it was in former times to believe that the divine might come down to earth in the disarming guise of a child. The apostle Paul, the messenger of this good news, wrote that the gospel was "a stumbling block to the Jews and folly to the Greeks" (I Cor. 1:23). This does not suggest that people were more credulous then than now or easier to convert.

The fundamental reason people in biblical times said that Jesus was the light of the world was that he showed them so much. The great achievements of Greek philosophy and science, which are still part of the foundation of our own civilization and valuable for understanding our universe, were like a candle to the light of the sun when compared to the understanding Jesus gave them concerning the great questions of life. In him they also found the Jewish expectations of a savior greatly surpassed. This understanding was not achieved immediately or easily. The New Testament clearly shows that Jesus had to make strenuous efforts to overcome frequent and deep misunderstandings by his listeners and first followers. But slowly their understanding grew, and within a few generations Jesus was seen as the crown and culmination of the finest insights of the ancient world. It was precisely because both the heart and mind were satisfied that so many ancient people received the benefits that the full wealth of conviction brings.

Jesus becomes our light when we study his life and teachings and let them illumine the world in which we live, allowing them to show us what is worth striving for and what is reliable and trustworthy.

In spite of the common perception that science excludes religion, it is increasingly being realized today that this is not so, and that the Christian religion was actually a major stimulus and ingredient in the origins of the scientific revolution of the seventeeth century. Furthermore, the recent findings of science, especially in cosmology, are highly consonant with the Christian conviction that the order of the universe is the result of divine wisdom. The working of the universe uncovered by our sciences goes very well with the notion of a God who "arranged all things by measure and number and weight" (Wisdom of Solomon 11:20). It is not conceptually difficult to think of this magnificently ordered universe as the work of a great intelligence.[2]

Nonetheless, the God of the Bible, who knows each of us by name and cares when even a sparrow falls, cannot be known only from the study of the created order. As John Turkevitch, formerly a professor of chemistry at Princeton University and also a Russian Orthodox priest, once commented, "It is not difficult to conceive of a God in a scientific universe, but such a God is a God of very large numbers."

Professor Turkevitch was alluding to such facts as the size of our galaxy in which light from the nearest star, traveling at the speed of 186,000 miles per second, takes nearly four and a half years to reach us. Our galaxy has billions of stars and it takes over 100,000 years for light to travel from one end of the galaxy to the other. It is only one of billions. "Galaxies are to astronomy what atoms are to physics."[3] As the psalmist put it,

> When I look at thy heavens, the work of thy
> fingers, the moon and the stars which thou
> hast established; what is man that thou art
> mindful of him, and the son of man that
> thou dost care for him? (Ps. 8:3-4).

Yet the psalmist was convinced that God did care because the psalmist believed that God had led his people out of slavery in Egypt into a promised land and had provided for them through the ages. Professor Turkevitch also is convinced that God is not just a God of large numbers, but that each of us is irreplaceable to God. His conviction is based on what Jesus Christ has shown us and done for us.

Our sciences and other ways of gaining knowledge reveal a great deal about the order and structure of the physical universe, the movement of history, the organization of societies, and the workings of the individual psyche. But none of these wonderful ventures of the human spirit are concerned with our *significance*. None of them can remove a moral failure that deeply injures another and destroys the joy of our life. None of them can inspire a life of concern and service to others. None of them can ease the cry of the heart at the death of a loved one nor comfort those who are afflicted. The greatness of Jesus is that he does speak to our deep, human concerns.

This book invites you to look at a person, Jesus of Nazareth, and to determine for yourself whether what he did and said satisfies your concern with the big questions of life and, indeed, with your own questions concerning the purpose and significance of your own life. It is my experience that however familiar his name and the outline of his life may be to us, every new examination of what he did and said is full of surprises and increases our appreciation of his greatness.

Perhaps the biggest barrier to a fuller recognition of what Jesus does and can do is that we measure his gifts in terms of earthly success. For many people the only knowledge of religion comes from the television screen or what they were taught as children. Religion is presented in the same way as commercials for exercise machines, diets, beauty products, cars, and beer. All too often the idea is conveyed that Jesus will help you overcome all your problems and enable you to become prosperous. This attracts some people; it repels others. In both cases what Jesus actually offers is missed.

Consider, for example, Mary Magdalene, one of Jesus' followers. Mary was a notorious person, an easy lay, as we would put it today. No one had any respect for her. However much our mores have changed, it isn't difficult for us to recognize that there is a very real difference between people of either sex who are grossly promiscuous and those who are not. In recent years biblical commentators have pointed out that, even though Mary Magdalene had been regarded throughout Christian history as a former prostitute, the biblical texts that refer to her do not explicitly say so. But whatever the case, Mary Magdalene's restoration was one of the great witnesses to Jesus' power, and Jesus's power to restore notorious prostitutes is evident in Luke 7:36-50, as we will later see. Jesus' power transformed Mary into a wholesome person that everyone could respect. Part of Jesus' greatness was his effect on her life, which was there for everyone to see. But more fully to appreciate the greatness of Jesus' power, we may contrast it to that of another great man, Socrates.

In Plato's dialogue, *The Symposium* or *The Banquet*, Socrates and some friends were discussing the nature of love when Alcibiades, one of Socrates' former pupils, barged into the dining room drunk as a lord. Alcibiades had been Socrates' most promising disciple—clever, handsome, well-connected. Now he was leading a life of dissipation. The setting of the dialogue is a flashback, so its readers know that soon after this meeting with Socrates, Alcibiades betrayed his country and, even worse, revealed the secrets of one of the mystery religions—considered to be the most despicable thing a person could do.

In the dialogue, Alcibiades lavishly praised Socrates, and explained how he had become Socrates' pupil or disciple. He said that he really could not explain Socrates' attraction. Socrates was not good looking and he spoke in the everyday language of the market place (somewhat as Jesus did) rather than with the impressive rhetoric of the famous teachers of the day. Yet he admitted, that somehow Socrates' words got into you. You could feel them swell like seeds that are starting to grow, and they made you want to change your life. Even as he spoke he said he could feel the rightness of Socrates' words and they made him feel ashamed of the way he lived. But it became clear in the dialogue that nonetheless Alcibiades was unable to change, and that however much Socrates cared for him and he for Socrates, Alcibiades was now beyond help because he had become corrupt. He was beyond the power even of Socrates' great wisdom and love.

People in ancient times feared corruption. Just as food can become spoiled so that it cannot be restored to wholesomeness, so too can people become so corrupt as to be beyond restoration. This is why Socrates, Plato, and Aristotle, the greatest philosophers of ancient times, feared easy pleasures. Children were carefully supervised because if left wholly to their own devices they would do whatever was fun. Easy pleasures, that did not develop character and self-discipline, were contrasted with higher pleasures that only came after the demanding effort of learning how to read or to play an instrument. Unless one has developed self-discipline, easy pleasures become addictive—the more you have, the more you want. When it is a choice between making an effort and an easy pleasure, the easy pleasure frequently wins. A person that follows this course finds that in time boredom becomes a serious problem. The demand for excitement becomes more and more insistent, and eventually erodes all self-restraint. In time all sense of propriety, and even the ability to direct one's own life are lost. Then one is unable to change without a great deal of help. Some people, like Alcibiades and Mary Magdalene, reach the point where no one can help them. It was said that Jesus cast seven demons out of Mary Magdalene. In ancient Israel seven implied totality, fullness, or wholeness. This is evident in the opening of Genesis where it is said that God created the heavens and the earth in seven days. In the case of demonic possession, seven signifies total, complete, or maximal possession.[4] This indicates the completeness of Mary's corruption and the completeness of her restoration.(Luke 8:2; Mark 16:9).

In *The Symposium*, Plato publicly admitted that Alcibiades had gone beyond the reach of the restorative power of Socrates, the person Plato most admired. In the New Testament, Jesus is portrayed as able to restore to wholesomeness those who had become corrupt. His parable of the prodigal son, who was restored to a place of honor by his father's power and love, was not just a story; it described something that Jesus himself could do, and something that people could see that he had done in the case of Mary Magdalene. She was a concrete reason for people to listen to him and to follow him. What Jesus did was beyond the power of the greatest philosophers and beyond the power of the greatest teachers of the Jewish Law. A popular fallacy that has only recently been discarded is that a really good psychiatrist has the knowledge and power to restore anyone to a normal, productive life, no matter what they have done and no matter what they have become. But those in the practice of psychiatric medicine know only too well that a great deal of human disorder is beyond their reach, just as a great deal is beyond the reach of non-psychiatric medicine.[5]

In this book we will examine what, according to the New Testament, Jesus did for people. Not everyone is like Mary Magdalene or the prodigal son. But everyone needs to lead the kind of life that Jesus made possible. Popular television religion appeals to our desire for earthly success or plays on our fear of hell (or both). I wish to correct this misrepresentation of Christianity by portraying the true benefits which following Jesus brings.

Because I spend so much of my time with academic people, who (rightly) are critically-minded, and because almost all educated people today are at least vaguely aware of disputes among biblical scholars about the Bible, I need to say a word about how I use the Bible in this book.

One of the most exciting discoveries of the Renaissance was that the Bible is a *historical* document. This does not mean that it was not inspired by God, but that it took centuries for it to achieve its present shape. The attempt to determine the steps and stages of its formation has shed a great deal of light on our understanding of God and of how God works with people through the centuries.

In the Gospels—the part of the Bible I shall appeal to the most—one of the main distinctions is between what took place in Jesus' life and ministry and the way the early Church came to regard Jesus *after* his earthly ministry. This distinction is one any of us ought to recognize in the case of our own lives. We know that the way we understand ourselves and events in our lives *as they are taking place* and the way we understand them *later* are not precisely the same. So too with Jesus' life.

Now the four Gospels were written from the perspective of how Jesus was understood *after* his earthly ministry was completed. They were not written from the perspective of how things seemed *at the time* to Jesus or to his companions or to those who were present on various occasions. There are glimpses of how things seemed at the time, but the Gospels were written with the full conviction that Jesus is Immanuel, God with us. This conviction is what they seek above all to portray. They also seek to help people understand it better and appreciate it more deeply.

The literary genre of biography had not yet been invented. But even if it had, it would not have been of any use to the Gospel writers. As Ludwig Wittgenstein, perhaps the greatest philosopher of this century, put it to a friend who was struggling to render the four Gospels into a harmonious, historical narrative, on the model of a modern biography:

> But if you can accept the miracle that God became a man all these difficulties are as nothing, for then I couldn't possibly say what form the record of such an event would take.[6]

It was not a Greek or Roman god taking human form for a while, but the awesome God of Israel, of whom no picture could even be imagined, that was said to *become* a human being. From a literary point of view, the four Gospels—Matthew, Mark, Luke, and John—are unique, newly minted works of art, which disclose to us the hitherto unimaginable world of God as it intersects our created world. Prosaic chronicles or even chaste modern historical renderings of Jesus' life would utterly fail to present the intersection of two worlds which Jesus, as the incarnate Word of God, is said to be. As this is increasingly appreciated, the achievement of the four Gospel writers becomes immensely impressive.

This by no means undermines the legitimacy or the value of biblical scholars' attempt to distinguish the way the early Church came to understand Jesus' life and achievements *after* Jesus' earthly ministry was completed from the way they were understood *as they were taking place*. This distinction is what is meant by "the quest for the historical Jesus." It is not that the Church's understanding is fantasy because it is not historical in terms of biblical scholars' reconstructive project, anymore than our understanding of our earlier life at a later time is fantasy. The search for the historical Jesus is pernicious only when the mere fact that a particular passage was written from a later understanding disqualifies it from being taken as a sound or true understanding of Jesus. The frequent comment by biblical commentators that a particular verse or title for Jesus is "a later addition" should not be taken to mean that it is automatically to be disregarded; that it cannot reveal to us who Jesus is and what he achieved.

In this book I present the early Church's understanding of Jesus' life, because so much of the significance of Jesus' life and ministry could not be grasped at the time the events transpired, but only afterwards with the benefit of reflection on his entire life. In other words, although I frequently use, without always mentioning it, many things that we have learned from a historical approach to the study of the Bible, my interpretations are ultimately based on the four Gospels as they are written, not as they are dissected.

A good summary of what biblical scholars presently think Jesus' life and ministry were like as they were taking place is given in an article in the *New York Times Book Review*, "Jesus Among the Historians" by John P. Meier, Professor of New Testament at the Catholic University of

America. From it we can see for ourselves that, however much we believe we can say about Jesus apart from the early Church's and four Gospel writers' understanding of him, such an approach does not enable us to consider what is important for us about Jesus as we try to make sense of life in general and our own lives in particular.[7]

I read the Gospels with the "eyes of faith." This means to read with the conviction that the Gospels give us access to the divine reality in which we live and move and have our being. It is to read the Gospels asking what God desires to show us about what we are to believe, do, and hope for. Rather than being contrary to the use of our minds, to read the Gospels with faith requires us to employ the results of a historical approach and whatever else from science, philosophy, and human experience that enhances our understanding. But unlike the academic study of the Bible, which does not require us to be guided or motivated by the conviction that Jesus is God incarnate, nor even require us to be concerned with the big questions of life, to read the Gospels with faith requires both this conviction and concern. A literary approach to the Gospels, favored today among Narrative Theologians, encourages us to read more closely to the way the Gospels are written than does the standard historical-critical method of biblical scholarship. But even so, a literary approach does not of itself require one to be guided by the conviction and concern that a believer has. It is because we have at least tasted the blessings that God seeks to bestow on us that we read the Gospels with faith, and thus discern what others do not see.

As Jesus said, "For to him who has will more be given, and he will have abundance; but from him who has not, even what he has will be taken away. This is why I speak to them in parables, because seeing they do not see, and hearing they do not hear, nor do they understand. . . .But blessed are your eyes, for they see, and your ears, for they hear" (Matt. 13:12-13, 16).

In my reflection on the greatness of Jesus as presented in the four Gospels, not every possible question about Jesus, God, and the Bible is examined. But then not every possible question about atomic particles is or has to be examined in a scientific paper for it to be convincing and worthy of acceptance. Enough will be said, I believe, to allow a person who seeks God to find God, and anyone who knows God to better know that inexhaustible source of goodness and life.

1. Yoder, Edwin. "Mourning Man's Last Sense of Wonder." Washington *Post* Writers Group, Dec. 25, 1987.

2. Allen, Diogenes., *Christian Belief in a Postmodern World*. Louisville, KY.: Westminster/John Knox Press, 1989. I fully argue the question of Divine Wisdom and modern science/technology in that book.

3. Sandage, Alan, *National Geographic Atlas of the World*. 5th ed. Washington, D.C.: Nat. Geographic Society, 1981.

4. Rengstorf, Karl. "Ἑπτά." (Hepta). In *Theological Word Book of the New Testament*. Gerhard Kittel, ed., G.W. Bromley, trans., vol. 2. Grand Rapids, MI: Eerdmans, 1987.

5. See, for example: Drury, M. O'C. *The Danger of Words*. London: Routledge and Kegan Paul, 1973.

6. ibid., xiii

7. Meier, John P. "Jesus Among the Historians." *New York Times Book Review*, Dec. 21, 1986.

CHAPTER ONE

A Monstrous Mistake

One day last winter I attended for the first time in years a Greek Orthodox service of worship. It is a wonderful but strange experience for people who are used to the simplicity of Protestant services. One stands before masses of pictures of saints, with a picture of Christ seated high on a throne in their midst, symbolizing that he is the source of all those wonderful lives around him, and indeed the source of the lives of those standing before him in the congregation. The priest, clad in magnificent vestments, faces the altar, preparing to celebrate the sacrifice of Jesus on the cross. The sound of the priest and cantors singing the service, and the fragrance of incense (symbolizing prayers of thanksgiving rising to God) fill the church with a sense of holiness. At a certain point in the service, a book that contains only the four Gospels is elevated before the people to signify that it is our source of the knowledge of Jesus—the way, the truth, and the life. Everyone stands while a passage is read aloud by a layperson. Although the church is aglow with light, when a passage of the Gospels is read, a person stands nearby, holding a large candle.

What struck me that day was the beautiful reverence and attention of the man holding the candle, listening to the Gospel passage about Jesus. He was from Uganda, a place where recently thousands of people have heard of Christ for the first time. It then struck me why a large candle is held to honor the reading from the Gospels. The candle means that Christ is the light of the world. There is a darkness, a great, deep darkness that envelops our hearts and minds, and Christ has come as a great light to dispel that darkness that we may live in the light.

But so many men and women today do not think of Christ as the light of the world. They do not think of themselves as being in darkness. We are enlightened people. Our museums and libraries are full of our discoveries. Schools and universities revamp their curricula every year or so because the material becomes out of date. Television shows us the wonders of space walks and close-ups of planets billions of miles away. Africans from Uganda, and the people of ancient Palestine when Jesus lived, perhaps they were in darkness. But not we today.

Yet most people have always felt that they were enlightened, whenever and wherever they lived. And indeed, were not the Romans enlightened? Had they not achieved as much or perhaps even more than any other people before them? They built great roads all across Europe and North Africa that were as straight as a yardstick, and were so durable that they lasted for hundreds of years. The beauty of their aqueducts and the magnificence of their buildings are still a source of inspiration for architects. Their brilliant administration of a vast empire allowed commerce to flourish, and thus provided the economic foundation for great centers of learning. They rightly felt

2

themselves to be an enlightened people.

Or consider the Jews of Jesus' day. They also thought of themselves as enlightened. Through Abraham they had a covenant, a sacred promise and relationship with God. Through Moses, God had revealed the Ten Commandments and many other laws. Because they knew the true God, they were to be a light to the nations.

And yet both the Romans and the Jews made a terrible, monstrous mistake. They, who knew so much, did not recognize the truth when they saw it. They did not recognize God's Word when it became a man, stood before them, healed their sick, comforted their weary, called their outcasts to his side, and put their children on his knee.

Consider Judas, who was one of the chosen twelve and who was present at the Last Supper. As he followed Jesus from place to place and listened to Jesus address the crowds, he must have become disappointed. For some reason or other, Jesus failed to live up to his expectations. So he betrayed his friend in a dreadful way: In the darkness of the garden of Gethsemene he revealed to the authorities which of his group was Jesus by kissing him. Judas made a monstrous mistake. He thought he knew what he was doing. Actually, he was in a darkness so deep that he did not recognize the true light even when he had been so close to it.

The soldiers, who guarded Jesus after he was arrested, were brutal, but at least their behavior was more innocent than Judas'. They had not associated with Jesus and, because they were not Jews, they did not share the Jews' expectations. They were simply soldiers doing a dirty job in an alien land. They had to take their fun when they could get it. Their chance came when Jesus was turned over to them, condemned to die because he claimed to be a king. They put a purple robe around him—the mark

3

of royalty—and crowned him with a crown of thorns. Then in mockery they bowed, spat on him, and roared with laughter. Finally, they beat him. They made a terrible mistake.

Then there were the learned men of Israel, the chief priests and scribes. They were the guardians of all that had been learned about God; they had great expectations concerning what God would do. Throughout their history the Jews had been a people who had expected things from God. They had left Egypt with Moses expecting to find a new home, flowing with milk and honey, which God had promised them, and they had found it. Abraham had been promised that his descendants would grow into a multitude as numerous as the stars of the heavens, and they had indeed become a large race. God had promised them a Messiah, but they were not sure precisely what kind of Messiah to expect. Still, they looked for a Messiah and waited for his coming, and assumed that they would be able to recognize him on the basis of what they knew.

But when he came, the priests and scribes did not recognize him. They kept misunderstanding him. When he was friendly with tax collectors, such as Matthew and Zacchaeus; or when he helped prostitutes or the woman about to be stoned; or when he ate with common people, who were ritually unclean, they condemned his behavior. When he told Nicodemus, one of the learned leaders, that he needed to be born anew, Nicodemus replied, "How can a man be born when he is old? Can he enter a second time into his mother's womb and be born?" (John 3:4). He completely misunderstood.

Jesus so upset most of the Jewish leaders that eventually they decided that they would have to get rid of him. They arranged to arrest him by bribing Judas. Then they had some people testify against him at a trial, but couldn't get the testimony to agree. Finally, when he was bluntly asked, he told them who he was. But they still did not recognize him. Rather, they took his statement as conclusive evidence of his blasphemy. The next day they took him to Pilate, the Roman governor, who alone had the power to put people to death. As John so simply but painfully put it, "He came to his own home, and his own people received him not" (John 1:11).

How could this monstrous mistake have happened? How could they have failed to recognize him? Indeed, how can God keep coming to *us* and we not recognize God's presence in our lives? For just as many people in Jesus' day failed to see in him the wisdom of God, so too do we all too often fail to recognize God's presence in our lives. This happens to us even when we have made a commitment to follow Jesus. The failure of so many Romans and Jews to recognize who Jesus was should not make us scorn them. It should serve as a warning that we too can very easily fail to recognize who Jesus is, and even if we do, very easily fail to be properly affected by him.

Consider, for example, the candid remarks of Austin Farrer about his attitude toward his fellow teachers at Oxford University.

> I believe in Jesus Christ, born, suffering, risen; yet I may leave the desk for the table, and find in my fellow diners the objects of my rivalry or the sources of my amusement, but never see the Christ in their hearts, or acknowledge in mine the Christ who goes out to meet them. . . . Our creed shows us the truth of things, but when shall we attend to the truth it shows? The life of the world is a strong conspiracy not of silence only but of blindness concerning

the side of things which faith reveals. We
are born into the conspiracy and reared in
it, it is our second nature, and the Christianity into which we are baptized makes
little headway against it during the most
part of our waking hours.[1]

Farrer describes a familiar experience. So much of the
time we live as though Jesus had never existed. There are
few things to remind us of him in the accepted social
customs of daily life. It was not just during Jesus' earthly
ministry that people failed to recognize him as Immanuel,
God with us. Even today when this is taught by the New
Testament and the Christian churches, it is either ignored
or, when it is accepted, not properly acted on. Perhaps the
most important reason is our expectations.

Expectations are crucial. One of the major reasons for
disappointment among college students is that they have
the wrong expectations about college. One major source of
difficulties in marriage is the divergent expectations of the
partners. Likewise in experimental science expectations
can cause us to misinterpret the results of an experiment.
But expectations can also be a reason for success in college
and in marriage. In science expectations enable us to
recognize the truth when we see it. What is important is to
have the *right* expectations.

One of the reasons we find it difficult to accept Jesus as
we ought is that we do not realize that God takes us as
seriously as God does. We do not really think that God has
made each one of us in the divine image and that, for this
reason, God expects a great deal of us. It is not at all
obvious that we do bear God's image. People do terrible
things: lie, steal, neglect children, and even kill brutally.
We know only too well that we ourselves are all too often

jealous, envious, and hateful, sometimes unable even to show common courtesy. How can we possibly believe that every one of us is made in God's likeness?

Teresa of Avila, the sixteenth century Spanish spiritual reformer, has a wonderful explanation for the paradox that we, who do so many terrible things, nonetheless bear the divine image. In her book, *The Interior Castle*,[2] she compares the human personality to a castle that has many rooms. The central room is the image of God (I have modified her allegory, but the sense is the same). Although we live in the castle, many of us never live in that particular room. Rather, we have smeared it with dirt and in other ways defaced it. When we look at each other and at ourselves in moments of honest self-examination, what we see often disappoints us and sometimes even revolts us, because we do not see the image of God but only the way we have defaced it.

Nonetheless, the teaching that we are made according to the image of God sometimes moves us deeply because at times we feel that we are significant. When people treat us badly, we want to cry out, "That isn't fair. I should not be treated this way. It is outrageous!" But even though we sometimes feel this truth in our hearts and voice it in our distress, most of the time we dismiss these stirrings as an illusion.

Yet we do bear the image of God, however much it is defaced. Those feelings are grounded on the bedrock of reality. Even though we are not living the life for which God made us, we are able to do so. Teresa of Avila tells us that the entrance to that "room" is prayer. This is why Austin Farrer turns immediately to prayer after his description of his blindness to the image of God in his colleagues. In prayer he recalls "the truth which Jesus died to tell, and rose to be." He finds himself asking,

What could I have been thinking? What
have I been missing? How could I be such
a fool, to forget Jesus in my friends, and to
see them as so many claimants, rivals, bores,
obstacles, instruments?

He then adds:

[Because of this self-examination] we are
broken-hearted and then we rejoice; broken-hearted at what we have refused to
see, but rejoicing more, because we see it;
and we go on in our prayer to express some
rudiments of love for our neighbor and our
God, and to devise some way for giving
that love effect.

Jesus is the image of God in a way that we are not.
Unlike us, he actually lived the kind of life God intends all
of us to live. He realizes, or actualizes, the image. This is
why attention to his earthly life is so important. We see in
him what we are expected to become, but have not become. Indeed, we have so injured ourselves that we cannot
become like Jesus without help. We are dependent on
God. This is why Teresa of Avila said that the entrance to
the "room" is prayer.

It is only by calling on God that we are enabled to pierce
the darkness that so pervades our hearts and minds that
we are unable to receive the truth of what we and others
are. Contact with God's gracious love enables us to live by
the light shed by that truth. By receiving God's love for us,
we can begin to live the life that God intends us to live.

Unless we have entered that "room"—begun to live the

life God intends us to live—the teaching that we are made in the image of God simply does not ring true. A casual glance at people is enough to make us dismiss it as sentimentality—the result of thinking with the heart, not the head. As a consequence, we are unable to recognize the greatness of Jesus as actualizing the image of God in his life. We are in the ranks of those who turned away from Jesus' teachings, rather than among those disciples who, when asked by Jesus whether they too wanted to leave him, replied "Lord, to whom shall we go? Your words are words of eternal life" (John 6:68, NEB).

It should be emphasized that the word "life" in the original Greek is *zoe*, rather than *bios*. *Bios* means biological life, implying existence as a plant or as we would put it today, to live like a vegetable. *Zoe* denotes the uncreated life of God. God wants to draw us into that life. *Zoe* is eternal life, a life inspired by and filled with God's Spirit. God takes us so seriously that God goes to the unprecedented lengths of becoming a human being for our sake. God actualizes the divine image for us in a human life, and assists us through example, teaching, and contact with his merciful love to realize it ourselves.

God's very coming in human form shows that each of us is irreplaceable. Rather than discarding us for our failure to live up to what we were intended to be, he comes to restore us. This is implied in Jesus' parable of a shepherd who lost one sheep out of a herd of a hundred. The shepherd is not satisfied to possess the rest of the herd, but goes in search of the lost one. When he finds it, he "calls together his friends and his neighbors, saying to them, 'Rejoice with me, for I have found my sheep which was lost'". Jesus then draws the parallel, "Just so I tell you, there will be more joy in heaven over one sinner who repents than over ninety-nine righteous persons who need no repentance" (Luke 15:6-7). Rather than being satisfied with what he has and cutting his losses, so to speak, God seeks each one of us because each one of us matters to God.

In Jesus' day many shepherds were not the owners of the herds they tended. In general, shepherds had a bad reputation for neglect and dishonesty. For example, shepherds would report a lamb as eaten by wolves rather than admit that it had been lost, or even sold by them for slaughter. Jesus' parables have been so successful in changing our image of shepherds that we no longer realize how startling is his teaching that God is not neglectful but goes out and searches for each of us.

It is the divine love that makes each one of us of irreplaceable value. Without that love, we would not be. Only some of us are accomplished, highly intelligent, good looking, and the like. In a loving family the various members are not cared for because they are more accomplished, more intelligent, or better looking than people outside the family. Similarly we are not irreplaceable to God because we are superior in some fashion to other people. We are irreplaceable to God because of the blessing God *wants to give all of us*. Because he *so* loves us he wants each of us to enjoy the kind of life that Jesus enjoyed. We catch a glimpse of the wonder of God's gift when we see the immense gratitude of the tax collector Zacchaeus, who in his joy publicly announced, "Behold, Lord, the half of my goods I give to the poor; and if I have defrauded any one of anything, I restore it fourfold" (Luke 19:8). We glimpse it also in Farrer's release from the limitations of the daily attitudes he has toward others when he sees them and himself in the light of God's love.

However much we hear today that there is a plurality of values, the value of every human being is assumed by every major ethical theory in western culture. It underlies the world-wide appeal to human rights. But it has been forgotten that its basis is the divine love as revealed by Jesus. Jesus' treatment of lepers, women, children, tax collectors, "sinners" (people who did not obey the ritual demands of the Jewish law as it was understood in Jesus' day), gentiles (non-Jews, such as the Roman soldiers who occupied Palestine), Samaritans (those Jews who were shunned by the supporters of the Temple cultus) is unprecedented.[3]

It is very easy to be sentimental about love and thereby completely misunderstand the nature of God's love. Consider, for example, a man who abandoned his wife and children to take up with another woman. After a few weeks, he telephoned his sixteen year old daughter. He said, "I just wanted to tell you that I love you." If the love he felt was a Christian love, the kind of love God seeks us to have, then the natural response of his daughter would have been, "O wonderful! When are you coming back home?" But that is not what he meant when he said that he loved her. He wanted to keep on doing precisely what he was doing and for her to think well of him so he would not feel so guilty.

Christian love does not allow us to do anything we feel like doing. It rules our life: that is, it orders and shapes our life so that should we do another person harm, such as the harm done to the girl by her father, we deeply regret it. As Austin Farrer put it once in conversation, a saint is not a person who stores up good, but one who, when he or she does wrong, repents immediately. A sentiment that makes us glow and, by its warmth, allows us to deceive ourselves about what we are doing, is not the love that God sheds abroad in our hearts. We are required to live as we ought to live and, whenever we fail, we are to repent and earnestly seek to mitigate as much as we can the harm we have done.

I expect most people find such words as "rule," "order," and "repentance" repulsive. Because of their initially negative ring, we often fail to look more closely and learn what they mean on the lips of Jesus. We then fail to recognize who Jesus is and to understand what he does for us, so that we never find the joy of the kind of life God seeks us to have and we never recognize our own greatness. The image of God we bear remains hidden from our sight and we fail to experience our own irreplaceable value.

When we carefully study the meaning of the words "order," "repentance," "judgment," "punishment," "suffering," and the like we realize the incredible lengths to which God is willing to go to enable us to actualize our greatness, and also the lengths to which we must go to reach our full and rightful stature. We too easily make the terrible mistake of selling ourselves short and settling for far less than God wishes us to have. It is no accident that there are so many instances of people who are described as joyful in the Gospel stories. That is the effect Jesus had on them. But to enter into that joy one has to get beyond the barrier of words like "order" that sound so negative. Our situation reminds me of that dreadful moment when, as a boy, I stood on the high diving board at our local swimming pool, trying to get my nerve up to jump for the first time. How quickly that dread turned to exhilaration when once I jumped. What had looked so hard and awful, now seemed so easy and so much fun.

Not all of the Christian life is exhilarating. There are a lot of obstacles to be overcome on the journey from where we are to where we are to be. This is why the word "suffering" occupies such a central place in Christianity, as we shall see. But it would be utterly untrue to the Gospel stories if the exhilaration at the first entrance to that "room" were left out of the account. And there is not only exhilaration at the beginning, but also everlasting joy at the end of the journey. We must now attend to some of those unattractive words so that we may find that "room" and begin our journey into everlasting joy.

1. Farrer, Austin *Lord, I Believe*. Cambridge, MA: Cowley Publications, 1989: 9-10.

2. Teresa of Avila. *The Interior Castle*. K. Kavanaugh, O. Rodriguez, trans. New York: Paulist Press, 1979.

3. Secular humanists, who explicitly reject Christianity, nonetheless take it for granted that every person has value and significance. They do not realize that without Christian convictions it is impossible to maintain that every human being has indefeasible value. (See, for example, Basil Mitchell. *Morality: Religious and Secular*. Oxford: Oxford University Press, 1980), and Glenn Tinder "Can We Be Good Without God?" Atlantic Monthly (December, 1989). 69-85.
Humanism, in contrast to secular humanism, is concerned with the value of *general* culture, rather than academic specialization and vocational education. Commitment to humanism (or humane studies) does not require one to oppose or to have a religious commitment.

CHAPTER TWO

Finding Our Place

Personal freedom has grown enormously during the last few centuries, and all over the world people strive for greater opportunities and personal liberties. The word "order" has become offensive to our ears largely because some governments use the need for order as an excuse for repression. Order is also usually associated with obedience to an authority. This can lead people to think that to obey Jesus and to recognize his authority destroys our freedom. But this is superficial. Almost every activity we value is based on a respect for order.

Consider, for example, science. The scientific revolution in the seventeenth century has enabled us to harness natural forces to serve our purposes in unprecedented ways. To mention only a few, electric lights have replaced candles, cars have replaced horses, and controlled environments now mitigate unpleasant weather. If nature were not orderly, we could not use it for our purposes. Order in science is equivalent to rationality, a very positive sounding word; disorder is associated with irrationality.

To become a scientist we must for a time accept the authority of practicing scientists. Of course, we sometimes feel resentful. But at other times we enjoy our increasing mastery of a subject or technique, and we realize that the freedom such knowledge gives us is worth the price of self-discipline.

In ancient times law-givers were highly honored as benefactors because it was generally recognized that the only way civilized life was possible was through obedience to laws. Good laws permitted a better common life. The ancient Athenians considered Solon to be one of the Seven Sages, the seven wisest men in history, because they thought that the splendid life they enjoyed was largely the result of the constitution devised by Solon at the foundation of the city.

Moses' place in Jewish history is as a law-giver. Unlike the Athenian law, however, the Jewish law is a gift from God *through* Moses. However much credit was given to Moses' leadership, human wisdom was not thought to be sufficient for discovering those laws that allow human communal and personal life to prosper *as fully* as God intends. The Jews symbolized this conviction in the story of the tower of Babel (Gen. 11:1-9). In this story all human beings shared a common language. Their ability to cooperate took a destructive form. They sought to build a tower that would reach the heavens to show that they were so powerful that they could do anything they wished. Their refusal to recognize their place in the order resulted in disorder, symbolized by their loss of a common language. Pride in our ingenuity is one of the sources of our present ecological crisis. Rather than increasing our respect for nature, scientific discoveries have far too frequently increased our abuse of nature.

Over the years the Jewish law was elaborated until it covered every detail of life, whether it be the preparation of food or the order in which sandals were to be put on. Through observance of the law, every Jew would be constantly reminded that he or she belonged to God. The same principle is present in Christianity. Practices, such as Bible reading and prayer, are to remind us of God's goodness and purpose. Habitual reminders, as they are called in Christian spirituality, are to form or shape us until we are constantly aware of God.

Jesus and Paul criticized some of the interpretations of the Jewish law on the ground that they failed to realize God's purposes or even ran counter to them. For example, Jesus taught that it is permissible to heal people on the Sabbath (Luke 14:1-6), and that the Sabbath was made for our benefit. We are not to be harmed through observance of it (Mark 2:27). Paul emphasized that we are saved by Jesus' sacrifice of himself for our sake, rather than by observance of the law. These criticisms should not encourage Christians to neglect the need to become as moral a people as possible and to scorn such efforts as "mere humanism."

Our moral achievements can indeed lead to pride and make us think that we "have no need of a physician" (Luke 5:31). Jesus pointed this out in his parable of the Pharisee, who proudly thanked God that he was not as other people (Luke 18:9-14). But the love of God that forgives us our sins does not exempt us from moral obligations. Jesus clearly taught the validity of the morality inscribed in the Jewish law. "Whoever then relaxes one of the least of these commandments and teaches men so, shall be called least in the kingdom of heaven; but he who does them and teaches them shall be called great in the kingdom of heaven" (Matt. 5:19). It is Jesus' claim to have the authority to explain the meaning of the law that led to conflict between him and the scribes and Pharisees, not a claim to abolish the Jewish law.

Another activity that we value is art. It too is dependent on order. Whether it be music, architecture, dance, poetry, or painting, all art requires form. To learn to express oneself through art requires discipline. This is illustrated in Wagner's opera, *The Mastersingers of Nurnberg*. The hero, Walther, is in love with a young woman, whose father has promised her as a bride to whoever wins the coming mid-summer musical competition. To compete, a person must be a Mastersinger. Walther is rejected as a member of the guild because the song he submits to the Mastersingers violates the rules of musical form. Hans Sachs, alone among the Mastersingers, recognizes the beauty of Walther's effort, and offers some friendly and useful criticism to Walther.

Sachs then passes onto Beckmesser, Walther's arch-rival, a poem which Beckmesser does not realize was composed by Walther. Beckmesser, by slavishly adhering to the Mastersingers' rules, fails to express the spirit of the poem. Sachs calls upon Walther to sing. Walther's music, having benefited from Sachs' criticism, reveals the vitality and beauty of the poem. The Mastersingers simultaneously admit Walther to membership and award him the mid-summer prize. Form alone is not sufficient for art, but discipline and structure enable inspiration to come to its full expression.[1]

Religion and art are very closely related. For example, Greek drama and dance originally developed from the worship of Dionysius, and modern drama developed from church ritual. In the middle ages, Gothic architecture was the creation of Abbot Sugar, who was inspired by a

Christian interpretation of Plato.

In an interview in *The New Yorker* (December 15, 1986), Lincoln Kirstein maintained that for art to flourish it must renew from time to time its religious inspiration. Kirstein is one of the most powerful figures in American performing arts. He is best known for his partnership with George Balanchine in founding the School of American Ballet and the New York City Ballet. But this is only one facet of his activity. There are some 473 items listed in his bibliography: fiction, poetry, drama, and books on drawing, painting, sculpture, architecture, photography, film, music, and literature. When asked to account for the source of his activity, he answered:

> Anybody who is interested in art has to realize that the great motor of art, over the last four thousand years, is religion. . . painting, architecture, and music—if you delete the religious principle from them you don't have anything. . . all art started from some kind of comprehension of cosmic order which they call religion, one way or another. It's discipline, and it's made incarnate in ritual. It's incarnate also in painting and architecture and music.[2]

In ancient Greece, Egypt, and Asia the order of the universe was thought to reflect the divine order. To participate in the cosmic order enabled one to participate in its divine source. Kirstein believes that religious ritual and genuine art seek to embody the cosmic order and thereby make its source or sources accessible to us. But, he continues,

At the present moment the organized religions are bankrupt; it is very hard for people
to get much satisfaction out of organized
ritual.

Although there has been a serious decline in church
attendance in most of Europe since the First World War,
and a slight decline since the mid-sixties in America, there
is also a widespread spiritual hunger. According to Kirstein,
art is also failing to assuage it.

The museums have been taken over by the
dealers, and the appreciation of art is really
the appreciation of negotiable value . . . .It
has nothing to do with the essentials of
what made art whatever it was for the last
two thousand years.

In contrast to the other arts, ballet has the advantage of being a group effort that demands great sacrifice.
But in general:

(There has been) a substitution of personal sensibility for a religious attitude. . .
and the canonization of the individual and
the fragmentation of skill and digital mastery. . . .
Modern art, as I see it, is nothing but a
terrible inflation of a kind of cancerous
self-indulgence. . . . Since the magic of
religion has disappeared, the magic of sensibility has taken over. And this is saleable.

For Kirstein, contemporary art does not embody the
cosmic order and thereby mediate its source or sources.

> How long do you suppose that an ordinary
> person stands in front of a picture to look at
> it? And there is a reason for it: there is
> nothing to look at. It's a superficial impres-
> sion of an image; all this comes back to the
> lack of any kind of essential interest in
> anything except oneself.

Even should one not share Kirstein's view that genuine art embodies the cosmic order and puts us into touch with its source or sources, the dependence of art on order is unassailable. In addition, it is clear that an appreciation of art has given many people a glimpse of what they considered to be precious, sustaining, enriching, challenging, elevating, and inspiring. This kind of appreciation requires "an essential interest" in finding a reality that transcends us as individuals. Without an essential interest, religious ritual is also superficial, rather than an opportunity for contact with the ultimate source of all that is valuable.

Let us consider more closely what is meant by "an essential interest." James Michener in his novel, *Hawaii*, describes the early missionaries' surprise at the interest shown by the native Polynesians in the genealogy of Jesus. That Abraham was the father of Isaac, and Isaac the father of Jacob, and Jacob the father of Judah, and Judah the father of Perez, and so on is perhaps the dullest part of the Bible. If one seeks to engage the interest of most readers today, Matthew's opening is certainly not a model to emulate. Why then did the Polynesians listen to it again and again with such interest? They had a genealogy of their own people which traced them through the centuries and specified their own place in the sequence of time and

21

place. It enabled them in effect to say, we are here, because there was a "before" that we can trace back from where we now are. They were rooted, rather than lost in the stars. There was an order and they had a place in the order. It transcended the individual and gave every individual a place. In addition, the stories associated with each name in their genealogy gave them guidance for their own lives, and the strength and confidence to face the future. They could be inspired to go forward because of all that they had been through as a people.

Because they had an essential interest in their place in the order, they listened with great interest to the genealogy of Jesus, to the stories associated with the various generations, and especially to Jesus' life. They soon incorporated their own history into the larger Christian order because it completed the understanding they derived from their own history.

Genealogy does not play an important part in most people's lives, nor is it necessary that it should. But it is important that we should have an interest in finding our place in a larger order. Without that interest most of the Bible is boring. The biblical past is not *our* past in the sense of giving our lives a "fix" in time and space. We are unable to draw upon that past, which is permeated with that which comes "from above," for guidance, strength, and hope. We are not part of what is larger and greater than ourselves. To the extent that we are interested only in ourselves, our present is a fleeting present, rather than one connected to what has gone before and directed toward a hopeful future. We become only a fleeting and narrow piece of consciousness, unaware of so much that is real and valuable.

Consider a story told by a teacher, who made a tour of England because of his interest in change bell-ringing.

Change bell-ringing is an English style of ringing a series of very large bells according to highly intricate sequences. Each bell has a single ringer, who must pull a bell-rope at precisely the right instant to fit into the sequence. The results of this physically and mentally demanding cooperative effort are far more beautiful than any individual could produce alone. It is musically much more accomplished than the simple tunes played by carillon bells.

On the train to the airport at the end of his tour, the teacher was disturbed by a couple of teenagers who had been to Europe for the summer. They were not only being loud and obnoxious, squirting sodas at each other, but they were utterly unaware of the lovely and historic countryside through which the train was passing. As a teacher, he was deeply concerned that they did not even realize what they were missing. Perhaps because of his recent experience of bell-ringing, he asked himself, "How will they find their place in the order?"

Change bell-ringing is a parable of life. It requires the acceptance and subordination of oneself to an order. So, too, does every other worthwhile activity. Participation in an order, whether through the scientific study of the natural world, taking part in community life, or the creation and appreciation of art, can point one to the ultimate source of all freedom and order.

To find our place in the proximate order is not always easy, and it is also not an ultimate resolution of life's quest, as T. S. Eliot discovered. He poses the problem in the second of his *Four Quartets*, "East Coker." Like the Polynesians, Eliot had an essential interest in his roots. East Coker in the west of England is the ancestral village of the Eliots. In the quartet "East Coker" Eliot explores the possibility that we can find a sufficient nourishment by establishing a connection to our social roots.

Eliot quotes the motto attributed to Mary, Queen of Scots, "In my beginning is my end." He uses the word "end" in the ancient Greek sense of "eschaton," meaning "last things" or "what is final," and "beginning" in the sense of "arche," meaning principle from which all else flows, as in the principles of geometry. According to the motto, our end is present at the very start of our life in the principle of our being.

If the principle of our being is our ancestors, then our end is the same as theirs, death. The dominant theme of the first part of "East Coker" is decay, and the peasants' dance is a dance of death. Eliot will become part of the earth, just like his ancestors. Eliot then explores another possibility. If the image of God is also part of the principle of our being, our life has a different end than the earth. He concludes his reflections in "East Coker" with an affirmation, which is the reverse of the motto of Mary, Queen of Scots, "In my end is my beginning."[3]

Our end is to realize the image of God. Each time we discern what we are to become is a new beginning. Every time we obey Jesus, who actualized the image of God, we reject a life style that leads to death as our ultimate end, and find our rightful place in the ultimate order. To obey Jesus is to enter the way that leads to the uncreated life, *zoe*, and to know that one does have a place in the order.

The journey is quite lengthy, however, because we need to be reshaped in so many ways to conform to the likeness of God in Christ. Perhaps the greatest single obstacle is our own rebelliousness. We resent many of Christ's commands and to follow him seems to cause us to miss a great deal of the fun other people have. This is well captured by the seventeenth century poet, George Herbert, who in his poem "The Collar," compares life under God to an actor on a stage ("the board") who cannot speak his own lines or do as he wishes but must follow a script.

> I struck the board, and cried, No more.
> I will abroad.
> What? shall I ever sigh and pine?
> My lines and life are free;

The rebel grows more and more incensed as he recalls all the pleasures he has missed because of his obedience. But he also exaggerates, until he is called back to his senses by recalling God's kindness.

> But as I rav'd and grew more fierce and wild
>   At every word,
> Me thoughts I heard one calling, *Child*:
> And I replied, *My Lord*.[4]

To be called a child and to suggest that we should reply "Lord" is extremely offensive to us because we are used to a great deal of personal liberty. Herbert's outlook smacks of the worst of authoritarianism and paternalism, which are very alien to the democratic spirit that has shaped us. Hierarchy in any form is widely said to be a perversion of Christianity which must be purged.

There is, however, such a thing as a perversion of the democratic spirit. Plato, who was well acquainted with democracy, points out its tendency to degenerate into anarchy because the people who found a democracy are not the people who live in it. The founding fathers of the American Constitution, recognized and tried to live up to the principles and values which commanded their allegiance. They recognized something that was higher than themselves. With each succeeding generation the stress on personal freedom and equality has grown stronger and stronger compared with respect for principles and values that transcend the individual. Since everyone enjoys doing as he or she pleases, unless the principles and values that transcend the individual are understood, they seem arbitrary and illegitimate restrictions. The cry for liberty and freedom from oppression becomes more and more common as the degree of self-discipline decreases. There is a tendency toward permissiveness, since there are no standards to which all of us ought to conform. Without standards, all pleasures and activities are equal and each person is free to do as he or she likes. Even to believe that there are or might be any standards to which our behavior ought to conform is thought to smack of authoritarianism. As Plato put it,

> If anyone says to him that some pleasures are the satisfactions of good and noble desires, and others of evil desires, and that he ought to use and honour some and chastise and master the others—whenever this is repeated to him he shakes his head and says that they are all alike, and that one is as good as another.[5]

This is precisely Lincoln Kirstein's lament:

> People rarely make any kind of qualitative judgments; they are not capable of it, any more than they make qualitative judgments about music or anything else for that matter. . . .How do you have the right to make a qualitative judgment? Alfred Barr, at the Museum of Modern Art, handled that marvelously. He never made a

qualitative judgment; everything is equally interesting.

Plato pays tribute to the positive aspect of the democratic spirit. The stress on personal freedom leads to a society with more variety than usual. But to maintain a society in which there is great personal freedom requires self-discipline, and that is harder for each generation to acquire. Eventually, more and more people are not able to live consistently. As Plato put it, one day a person is training hard in the gym, and the next he is debauched at a party. In time "his life has neither law or order; and this distracted existence he terms joy and bliss and freedom."

According to the founders of American democracy, to do whatever you like whenever you like is not a principle of democracy. They believed in moral principles that were higher than any individual's wishes. Unrestrained personal freedom assumes that there are no genuine standards of good and evil that have legitimate authority over us. Freedom, when understood to imply that there is nothing higher than our personal preferences, limits rather than liberates.

Jesus pointed out to his listeners that his teachings were not a matter of personal preference. A house without foundations, he said, will be swept away by heavy rains. But what he teaches provides a foundation for life that is so strong that nothing can sweep it away. (Luke 6:47-9).

Jesus impressed everyone with his authority. As a teacher of the Jewish law, he was called "Rabbi" or "Master." Unlike other teachers, however, he did not cite earlier teachers of the law, whose interpretations were regarded as authoritative. Rather, he spoke as one who himself had the authority to teach the will of God. When he did cite a source, it was from the Old Testament, and not other teachers' interpretations of it. People were astonished. Some, however, were resentful, and many who showed outward respect were not about to do as he taught. We find Jesus complaining, "Why do you call me 'Lord,' 'Lord,' and not do what I tell you?" (Luke 6:46).

Luke reports that immediately after this a centurion, whose slave was ill, appealed to Jesus for help. He was not put off by Jesus' claim to have authority. As a centurion, he himself had authority. It was conferred by a higher authority. He commands, but in the name of the Emperor, and in order to achieve the Emperor's aims, not his own.

The centurion recognized that the same sort of thing was true of Jesus. Jesus had received his authority from the God of Israel. But that recognition put him in a bind. He was not a Jew. Therefore he asked the elders of the synagogue in Capernaum to act as his intermediary. He reasoned, "I cannot go to him myself. But if you ask him, perhaps he will come to me, even though I am not a Jew."

The elders were glad to help him because, as they put it to Jesus, "He loves our nation and he built us our synagogue" (Luke 7:5). Word was sent to the centurion that Jesus was on his way. But the centurion became overwhelmed with embarrassment. He sent friends to Jesus with the message,

> Lord, do not trouble yourself, for I am not worthy to have you come under my roof; therefore I did not presume to come to you. But say the word, and let my servant be healed. For I am a man set under authority, with soldiers under me: and I say to one, "Go," and he goes; and to another, "Come," and he comes; and to my slave, "Do this," and he does it. (Luke 7:6-8).

Just as Solomon knew that God could not be contained by the majestic heavens, let alone by the magnificent temple he had built, this centurion knew that the synagogue he had built did not make him worthy to have Jesus enter his house. Yet like Solomon who asked God to hear the prayers of the people who came to the Temple, the centurion asked Jesus only to speak his saving word. (I Kings 8:22-3, 27-30, 41-3.)

Jesus marveled at this man's trust. He told the crowd that was following him that not even in Israel, where he would have expected it, had he found such faith. The centurion was familiar with authority and knew what those with authority could do. He recognized the authority of Jesus' very words. Jesus could heal the servant by the God given authority of his words just as God created the heavens and the earth by the pronouncement of his Word. Luke clearly means to show in this story that if we trust Jesus' words, we have a foundation for life which nothing can undermine. His words have the authority of God, whose words laid the foundations of the heavens and earth. Jesus' teachings are not arbitrary, but are to help us find what is worthwhile in life and to raise us to a higher level of life. The Latin root of "authority" and "authentic" means "that which allows growth and life." Our resentment of the authority of God in Christ is, therefore, foolish.

What can help us recognize the folly of rebellion against God? For some people it is the realization that, even though there are many delights in earthly life which God wants us to enjoy, in the last analysis, they do not satisfy. George Herbert describes it in his best known poem, "The Pulley".

When God at first made man,
Having a glass of blessings standing by;
Let us (said he) pour on him all we can:
Let the world's riches, which dispersed lie,
    Contract into a span.

So strength first made a way;
Then beauty flow'd, then wisdom, honor,
        pleasure:
When almost all was out, God made a stay,
Perceiving that alone of all his treasure
    Rest in the bottom lay.

For if I should (said he)
Bestow this jewel also on my creature,
He would adore my gifts instead of me,
And rest in Nature, not the God of Nature:
    So both should losers be.

Yet let him keep the rest
But keep them with repining restlessness:
Let him be rich and weary, that at least,
If goodness lead him not, yet weariness
    May toss him to my breast.

The same conviction is expressed on the opening page
of Augustine's *Confessions*, "Our hearts are restless until
they find rest in Thee." "Rest" is an allusion to the seventh
day of creation when, upon the completion of his work,
God rested. For us rest means that we no longer have to
search because we have found the source of fullness and
satisfaction.

We also may stem our rebellious moments by calling
upon God to help us in times of temptation. For example,

when people make us feel stupid because we pass up a chance for illicit sexual pleasure or fail to gratify our ambitions, God's authority reassures us of the soundness of our life. Herbert describes it in his poem, "The Quip."

> The merry world did on a day
> With his train-bands, and mates agree
> To meet together, where I lay,
> And all in sport to jeer at me.
>
> First, Beauty crept into a rose,
> Which when I pluckt not, Sir, said she,
> Tell me, I pray, Whose hands are those?
> But thou shalt answer, Lord, for me.
>
> Then Money came, and chinking still,
> What tune is this, poor man? said he:
> I heard in Music you had skill.
> But thou shalt answer, Lord, for me.
>
> Then came brave Glory puffing by
> In silks that whistled, who but he?
> He scarce allow'd me half an eye.
> But thou shalt answer, Lord, for me.
>
> Then came quick Wit and Conversation,
> And he would needs a comfort be,
> And, to be short, make an oration.
> But thou shalt answer, Lord, for me.
>
> Yet when the hour of thy design
> To answer these fine things shall come;
> Speak not at large, say, I am thine:
> And then they have their answer home.

One trusts God's assurance that life is to be found in obedience because one has already begun to share in God's life. Even though obedience to God means renouncing illicit pleasures, ill-gotten gains, and the vanity of social prestige, one does not have to waste one's breath trying to get back at those who scoff. Rather, when made fun of or when struggling with temptations, one may rely on the power of the very words of the Bible, "For in thee, O Lord, have I put my trust; thou shalt answer for me, O Lord my God" (Ps. 38:15), which Herbert uses in his poem. This can be verified in personal experience. When other people's worldly successes make you feel a failure, repeat the words of the Psalm or Herbert's paraphrase, and you will find yourself relieved of depression and resentment, and at ease.

Much of our difficulty is caused by distraction. Our earthly conditions keep us from fixing our minds on what is at stake. Herbert describes this in his poem, "Redemption," in which the speaker is concerned with the improvement of his earthly condition. He is disappointed that God has failed to provide him a better living. He seeks his Lord in those places which he believes provide the best kind of life—cities, theaters, gardens, parks, and royal courts. But he finds him in an astounding place, among thieves and murderers. His request is granted before he can even ask. Only then does it dawn on him that something far greater has transpired than he realized. He had to learn that for us to find fullness of life, God must suffer. Our thoughts and deeds are so significant that it took God's crucifixion to restore us to our place in God's order. To understand this profound truth we must examine more fully Jesus' teachings.

1. The opera, *The Mastersingers of Nurnberg*, was important to the development of Wittgenstein: "It was a treatment of problems of music and life at the same time—and its solution lay in the need for rules that can be discovered even within spontaneity but only when a note of reverence has been introduced. The opera contrives to show this . . . without overlooking the resignation and, from a human point of view, the loss involved in every achievement." McGuinness, Brian. *Wittgenstein: A Life.* Berkeley, CA: University of California Press, 1988. 55.

2. Lowry, W. McNeil. "Conversations With Kirstein:I."

3. Eliot, T. S. "East Coker." In *Four Quartets.* New York: Harcourt Brace Jovanovich, 1971.

4. Herbert, George. "The Collar." In *George Herbert.* John Wall, Jr., ed. New York: Paulist Press, 1981.

5. Plato's *Republic.* Benjamin Jowett, trans.; 1: New York: Random House, 1937, 1:819-20.

CHAPTER THREE

The Teachings of Jesus

Many of Jesus' teachings concern people who were excluded from the mainstream of society. In many cases it is easy to see why they were excluded. Thieves were criminals; prostitutes allowed themselves to be used to gratify lust; tax collectors overcharged because they were allowed to keep for themselves anything over their assigned quota; lepers were thought to be very contagious and therefore not allowed to live within towns or villages; people possessed by demons behaved abnormally and were sometimes violent. In spite of severe criticism from the religious leaders of the day, Jesus sought to restore these people to the larger community.

We have already seen that Jesus breached the barrier between Jews and Gentiles when he healed the centurion's slave and said of the centurion, "not even in Israel have I found such faith" (Luke 7:9). He also sought to overcome the barrier between Jews and Samaritans, whom the Jews considered to be heretical. In the parable of the Good

Samaritan, a Samaritan's action illustrates what it is to love one's neighbor as oneself, in contrast to the actions of orthodox Jews, a priest and Levite, who failed to help a man who had been robbed and left for dead by the side of a road. Jesus also dared to ask a Samaritan woman to draw him a drink from a well and publicly to engage in a serious conversation. When she reproached him, "How is it that you, a Jew, ask a drink of me, a woman of Samaria?" (John 4:9), he replied, "If you only knew who it is that is speaking to you" (John 4:10). In God's name he sought to remove whatever keeps us from living with each other as we ought.

The common people were referred to by the elite as "sinners." The scribes and Pharisees had so interpreted the Jewish law that it was impossible for ordinary people to earn a living and also observe the elaborate regulations that they devised. Simon Peter's first reaction to Jesus was, "Depart from me, for I am a sinful man, O Lord" (Luke 5:8). He probably meant that he was ritually unclean, not that he had serious moral failings. It was from these ordinary people that Jesus chose most of his closest disciples. He was so deeply aroused by the opposition of the scribes and Pharisees to his attempts to enlighten the common people about what God required that he told them, "You have taken away the key of knowledge; you did not enter [the kingdom of God] yourselves, and you hindered those who were entering" (Luke 11:52). But to the common people he said, "Come unto me, all who labor and are heavy laden, and I will give you rest. Take my yoke upon you, and learn from me; for I am gentle and lowly in heart, and you will find rest for your souls. For my yoke is easy, and my burden is light" (Matt. 11:29-30). He solemnly warned the scribes and Pharisees, "Temptations to sin are sure to come; but woe to him by whom they come! It would be better for him if a millstone were hung round his neck and he were cast into the sea, than that he should cause one of these little ones to sin" (Luke 17:1-2).

Most of us are not burdened by the Jewish law. But Jesus' teachings are still relevant. Divisions between nations, regions, social classes, rich and poor, employees and employers, family members, and within our own personalities are rife. Those who have a superior position are particularly prone to look down on others. But Jesus warns us that any one of us may be responsible for perpetuating barriers between ourselves and those who injure us. "Take heed to yourselves; if your brother sins, rebuke him, and if he repents, forgive him; and if he sins against you seven times in the day, and turns to you seven times, and says, 'I repent,' you must forgive him" (Luke 17:3-4).

When Jesus said this, his disciples were overwhelmed. They cried out, "Increase our faith!" (Luke 17:5). This seems entirely appropriate. Genuinely to forgive a person once is not always easy, and there are some people and some injuries we find it impossible to forgive. When we are faced with something that is difficult to do it is surely correct to ask for God's help.

Jesus' response to their appeal, however, was devastating. Increase your faith? Your problem isn't that you don't have enough faith, but that you don't have any. "If you did have faith, [even] as [little] as a grain of mustard seed, you could say to this sycamine tree, 'Be rooted up, and be planted in the sea,' and it would obey you" (Luke 17:6).

Is this literally true? If they had had even a tiny amount of faith, could they have uprooted a tree or, as Matthew and Mark put it, moved a mountain? Could we uproot a tree or move a mountain, if we had any faith at all? Is the ability to uproot trees and move mountains the mark of having faith? Is this the test of being a follower of Jesus?

Jesus does not ask us to believe that if we had faith we could uproot trees or move mountains. He makes a comparison of the difficulty of uprooting trees and moving mountains with the difficulty we have with forgiving each other and overcoming the barriers between us. We are not called upon to move trees and mountains. Rather we are to forgive each other's transgressions and to strive to remove vicious barriers that cause so much suffering, especially to those who are outside the mainstream of society or looked down on by others. The absence of an urgent desire to forgive and be reconciled is the sign of a lack of faith.

The issue, then, is not an increase of faith, but the very existence of any faith at all. The test is not whether we can uproot trees or move mountains, but whether we forgive those who repent of having injured us. We probably would rather have the mark of faith be that of uprooting trees and moving mountains because no one would really expect us to be able to do that. But forgiving each other is something people can do. Jesus tells us we can overcome many of the barriers between us if we have just a little bit of faith—faith in the way of life he reveals to us, faith in a generous God who does not place meaningless burdens on us. If we had such faith, it would then be appropriate for us to ask Christ to increase our faith, because there would be something for him to increase. We would also learn that we have a generous Lord who will enable us to perform the enormous feat of forgiving again and again as we grope our way through life, still not fully in control of our ambitions, jealousies, and pettiness.

Since Jesus said that we are to forgive even "seven times in the day," it suggests that he had in mind situations in which people are closely associated with each other, such as a family or place of work. Perhaps the disciples did not get along with each other all that well and were overwhelmed with his teaching. It is indeed life at close quarters which is probably the most severe test of faith. Can we really hope to overcome those deep barriers between husband and wife, parents, children, and siblings? But life at close quarters is also probably one of the most favorable places for faith to be increased. The life that is "from above," constantly offered, often becomes realized as the barriers between us are overcome and we enjoy life unhampered by so many negative attitudes. We come to believe more deeply in the life that God offers humanity because we have entered it ourselves.

In Jesus' warning to the scribes and Pharisees not to cause another person to stumble, there is a positive idea that we can apply to our lives. Sometimes the person we need to forgive stumbled because of us. Their repentance may open our eyes to the possibility that what they did to us did not come out of the blue, but resulted in part from our attitude and behavior. A repentant person might, therefore, provide an opportunity for us to take a step in the direction of the kingdom of God. Sometimes, however, our attempt to be reconciled with another is not successful. In these circumstances Jesus' words of welcome, "Come unto me, all who labor and are heavy laden" are very meaningful. His words are like a healing balm.

One of the reasons people go through life with unhealed resentments and cynicism about God's power to heal us is a lack of gratitude. Jesus teaches us that just as faith and forgiveness are connected, gratitude and forgiveness are too.

First he teaches us what gratitude looks like from the divine point of view, with a parable about a servant who came in from the fields after working all day

(Luke 17:7-10). He was ordered to prepare his master a meal. Jesus asked his listeners, "Is the master to be grateful that the servant does what he is commanded to do?" Rather shockingly he answered, "No". Therefore, when we have done all that is commanded of us, we are to say, "We are unworthy servants, we have only done what was our duty" (Luke 17:10). God is not grateful to us for our obedience in forgiving others, in becoming reconciled to others, as if we have done something extra special. This is perfectly compatible with the passage we mentioned earlier in which there is joy in heaven when a person repents. The joy is because one of God's lost creatures has entered the way that leads into never-ending life, not because God has received something above what is rightfully to be expected. We have only done what we are supposed to do— what people who have faith in God are supposed to do.

Then Jesus teaches us about gratitude from our vantage point. He met ten lepers who begged him to cure them. He told them to go and show themselves to the priests, who had the responsibility for certifying that healed lepers were free of the disease and no longer had to live apart from the community. As they went, they were cleansed. One of them, when he saw that they had been healed, turned back and, praising God with a loud voice, fell to the ground before Jesus, thanking him. Only one of the ten was grateful. Jesus then made a most revealing remark, " 'Were not ten cleansed? Where are the nine? Was no one found to return and give praise to God but this foreigner?' And he said to him, 'Rise and go on your way; your faith has made you well' " (Luke 17:17-8). The one with gratitude had been a double outcast, not only a leper, but also a Samaritan. It was because he believed in God that he recognized that his cleansing was a gift from God. To have faith is to be grateful to God for the good that comes our way. The other nine were healed, but they did not receive it as a gift from God. If they'd had faith, they would have.

People are bathed every day with God's good gifts. But all too often these gifts are taken for granted. They are not received as gifts from God at all. If they were, we would not only praise God, but we would seek to be reconciled with our brothers and sisters. For among the gifts of God is forgiveness which, when received and not taken for granted, makes us grateful. It makes us generous toward those who injure us and seek to be reconciled with us.

The Pharisees, who asked Jesus when the kingdom was coming, expected to be able to recognize the kingdom of God without being personally involved. Jesus sought to overcome their misunderstanding and said, "The kingdom of God is not coming with signs to be observed; nor will they say, 'Lo, here it is!' or 'There!' for behold, the kingdom is in the midst of you" (Luke 17:20-1). It is being created among us as we learn to be generous with each other because we have a generous Lord.

There is a price, then, even for those outside the mainstream of society, and those who suffer various disadvantages, for the gifts Christ offers. The kingdom cannot be taken for granted. Its reception is marked by gratitude toward God and generosity toward those who injure us. Jesus teaches us that it is worth the cost. He refers to the kingdom of God under the symbols of a treasure and a pearl of great value, and compares our situation to a man, who finds a treasure hidden in a field, "then in his joy goes and sells all that he has and buys the field" or to "a merchant in search of fine pearls, who, on finding one pearl of great value, went and sold all that he had and bought it" (Matt.13: 45-6).

The promise of a life free of destructive divisions is indeed glorious, but it still needs to be actualized. We are reluctant to do what it takes to actualize it; and this reluctance is especially noticeable among those who have a favorable social position. Consider, for example, the rich young man, who was so impressed with Jesus, that he ran up, knelt, and asked him, "Good Teacher, what must I do to inherit eternal life" (Mark 10:17).

Apparently, the young man was willing to conform to Jesus' teachings. Jesus began by correcting him. "Why do you call me good? No one is good but God alone" (Mark 10:18). God is the ultimate source of all goodness; all that is good relies on God's continuous activity. Jesus implied that everything that he has to give is from God. He was not acting and speaking in his own name, but with the authority of his Father. Then Jesus answered the young man's question by reminding him of some central commandments of the Old Testament; Do not kill; do not commit adultery; do not steal; do not bear false witness; do not defraud; honor your father and mother.

Since these are all Old Testament teachings, it suggests that not everything that we have learned in school and from our society about how we should live is necessarily wrong. Some of it may be sound. But it is not for us to decide on our own authority what is to be retained and what is to be discarded. The young man submitted all that he knew and all that he had become to Jesus' judgment. Even though he had apparently done everything Jesus endorsed since he was a youngster, he was not satisfied that he had done all that he needed to do in order to inherit eternal life. Having met Jesus, he apparently sensed that there was more to be done and more to be found.

Jesus encountered many people who were confident that the life they were leading was on the right track and that they were doing just fine. Jesus saw their self-righteousness and complacency. But this time it was different.

This young man was truly a fine person, so much so that Jesus, "looking upon him loved him, and said to him, 'You lack only one thing; go, sell what you have, and give it to the poor, and you will have treasure in heaven; and come, follow me'" (Mark 10:21-2).

This is an unprecedented honor. This young man had become so much like what we ought to become that he was invited to join Jesus' inner group, even though he had missed so much of the instruction that they'd, had. It seems that he had achieved so much that he could join them quite late in Jesus' earthly ministry without being at any particular disadvantage. But then with the invitation came a revelation. His expression changed and he went away sorrowfully because "he had great possessions."

In answer to the young man's question, Jesus did not mention four of the Ten Commandments which are about honoring God, and he expressed the commandment not to covet as a commandment not to defraud. The omissions and the alteration suggest that at first Jesus focused on the young man's actions. Only when Jesus told him to sell his possessions and to follow him did it become evident where the young man's allegiance lay.

He who had already achieved so much turned away sorrowfully, but nonetheless turned away. He is nameless to us, but he could have been as well known as Peter or one of the other apostles. Why would he not give up his possessions, and trust Jesus' promise of treasure in heaven? To have great possessions gives us social position. They elevate us over others. He apparently could not give up the social distinction and superiority that his possessions conferred.

Jesus calls us to renounce whatever we use to look down on others and in effect say, "I am not as others; a great chasm separates me (and those like me) from others." It may be wealth, good looks, brain power, physical strength, good health, an excellent job. In various respects some people have more than others. But none of these advantages puts anyone above others. We must renounce this use of our advantages. Otherwise we cannot follow Christ; we cannot find eternal life, or *zoe*, the uncreated life of God.

When Jesus' disciples heard Jesus say, "How hard it will be for those who have riches to enter the kingdom of God" (Mark 10:23), they were amazed. To fulfill much of the ritual and ceremonial law, as well as to be charitable, required substantial means. Besides, this young man was a splendid example of all that their religion had taught that a person should become. Nonetheless, Jesus stood firm. "Children, how hard it is to enter the kingdom of God! It is easier for a camel to go through the eye of a needle than for a rich man to enter the kingdom of God." (Mark 24-5). Jesus frequently used the well known teaching method of hyperbole, or exaggeration, to make a point. Rather than being a help, material wealth is a major obstacle to finding the rich, never-ending life offered to us by God. His teaching can be visualized through the image of a bird that is kept from flying freely by a single, silk thread tied to its feet. Even though a bird has wings and is in perfect health, it can flutter only a few feet off the ground as long as it has any attachment to the earth. Wealth can be like a silk thread for those who in so many ways are admirable people, but whose wealth keeps them from receiving the different kind of wealth to be found in God's kingdom.

The disciples, however, were baffled. "Then who can be saved?" (Mark 10:26). Jesus indicated that there are no natural means for achieving *zoe*. "With men it is impossible; but not with God; for all things are possible with God" (Mark 10:27).

The Spirit of God must find its way into us. To illustrate

this, John the Baptist forcefully contrasted his ministry to Jesus'. When people asked him what they should do in order to enter the kingdom of God, he told those who had two coats to share with those who had none. He told tax collectors to collect no more than they were supposed to. He told soldiers to be content with their pay and not use violence and threats to extort money. But then he made it clear that such repentance and baptism were only a preparation. "I baptize you with water; but he who is mightier than I is coming, the thong of whose sandals I am not worthy to untie; he will baptize you with the Holy Spirit and fire (Luke 3:16). John also speaks of unquenchable fire which will refine, burning all impurities away. This too suggests that to realize the image of God, we require God's help. The fire is not the threatening fire of hell, but the fire that is divine love. This is why it is unquenchable. It is God's love at work in us that burns away all impurities.

Even the finest and most remarkable of people need God. It is only by the presence of *zoe*, the undying life of God in us, that we can be free of those attachments that bind us to an earthly life. God's rich life in us is what enables us to be like the man who in his joy sold all he had to buy the field with a hidden treasure, or to be like the man who sold all his pearls because he found one pearl of great value. The rich young man was indeed seeking, but he was unable to recognize in what Jesus offered something worth giving everything else up for. God's gift remained hidden. From his sorrow we may infer that he at least sensed that he had missed something, but apparently this was not enough to enable him to exchange everything else for it.

It occurred to Peter that God must have been at work in him and the other disciples because, as he pointed out to Jesus, "Lo, we have left everything and followed you"

(Mark 10:28). Jesus agreed with Peter. This is remarkable because usually Peter got things wrong and had to be quite firmly corrected. But this was a notable exception. Jesus told his disciples that everyone who has left home, parents, brothers, and sisters for his sake would have them in abundance. This is apparently an allusion to the large following Jesus is building up. Everyone who follows Christ belongs to the great family he is creating.

We may draw a comparison between the disciples and those of us who follow Christ today. Even though not all of us have literally left all that we have to follow Jesus, many of us, as we grew up and were educated and formed by our society, did not choose the cheap and easy things of life. We pursued, as best we could, what was honorable, worthwhile, and wholesome. When we learned of Christ, each of us, quickly or gradually, joyfully responded to him. We were not like the rich young man, but in some measure at least we have been like the disciples who responded to Jesus' call to follow him.

But the story does not end at this point. As they were on the road that led to Jerusalem, a quarrel broke out among the disciples. Two of them had asked Jesus, "Grant us to sit, one at your right hand and one at your left hand, in your glory" (Mark. 10:37). The other disciples became indignant. We here realize that although they had left all else behind to follow Jesus, they still had the same desire that had kept the rich young man from following Jesus, namely the desire to be above other people. Although the disciples had followed Jesus, they had not left this desire behind. So when Jesus had quieted them down, he explained to them "You know that those who are supposed to rule over the Gentiles lord it over them, and their great men exercise authority over them. But it shall not be so among you; but whoever would be great among you must be your servant,

45

and whoever would be first among you must be slave of all. For the Son of man also came not to be served but to serve, and to give his life as a ransom for many" (Mark 10:42-5).

This is a revolutionary understanding of power and authority. They are not to be used to elevate oneself through the subordination of others. Rather, the power and status one has are to be used to serve others. Jesus teaches us that it is Godlike to serve. We honor God, not only because of God's majesty, but because God in Christ shares his way of life with us. In so far as we serve others, we share in God's life. In our service to others we are not to allow other people to take advantage of us, as if to be servile is to follow Christ. This would be to cast "pearls before swine" who do not appreciate the value of what we are doing (Matt. 7:6). We are to be "wise as serpents and innocent as doves" (Matt. 10:16).

To raise, lift, and encourage people is the mark of true greatness. To be in the kingdom of God is to seek good for other people. All of us have different roles in society. What we must give up is not necessarily what we have—our jobs, our position, our possessions—but the desire to establish ourselves over others. We are to use our possessions and position in a spirit of concern for others, as we see in Jesus' parable of the talents (Matt. 25:14-30). There is no competition in service in order to achieve a higher rank. We are to serve, not so as to establish ourselves over others, but because we care. The divine life—the purifying love of God that reshapes, remolds, and motivates us—is what enables us to care. The love that flows from the divine life at work in us is free of envy. It enables us to rejoice in people's service and to honor them for it as servants of God.

From this quarrel among the disciples, who had the

benefit of Jesus' teachings and company, we realize how deep our bondage to our self-concern is. Jesus emphasizes the danger of wealth because wealth to us means the ability to gratify our desires. It can prevent a fine person, such as the rich young man, from following Jesus. But even those without wealth can be blind to presence of a Christlike life. This is marvelously presented in a scene in Anthony Trollope's novel, *The Warden*,[1] written during the heyday of nineteenth century attacks on privilege.

The scene took place in a small almshouse in a rural part of England. The endowment for the almshouse maintained twelve retired craftsmen and a warden. The warden, who was an elderly, devout clergyman, was singled out for attack by a sensationalist national newspaper. The editor argued that the purpose of the almshouse was to provide for those in need, yet most of the endowment was earmarked for the warden. Even though the warden had the legal right to remain, he decided to resign his post and take a much poorer living. He arranged for the endowment that was earmarked for a warden's salary to be divided among the members of the almshouse. Once the members of the almshouse realized how much the warden meant to them, their spokesman pleaded with him to remain. But the warden firmly refused to reconsider and proceeded to resign.

On the last day of his office in a scene reminiscent of the Last Supper, the warden entertained the members with a marvelous feast. One of the inmates was bedridden, and the warden visited him in order to share a farewell glass of wine. In a hoarse voice he asked the warden, "It's true, then, that you're leaving?" "Yes, old friend it is true," replied the warden. At this the old man's eyes lit up as he asked, "When will we get the money?"

Since he was at death's door and without family, the

money would be of no use to him. But even more significant was his blindness to the fact that no amount of money
could buy the friendship and concern that the warden had
for him. Yet the money to him represented wealth, and the
notion of wealth so possessed him that he could not realize
what he was losing in exchange. Like Judas, who ex-
changed what Jesus had to offer for thirty pieces of silver,
the old man failed to receive the riches of a godly affection.

We can become possessed not only by avarice, but also
by such things as lust, envy, pride, hatred. For example,
when we are filled with hatred, no matter what the person
we hate does, it feeds the fires of rage and scorn. We
become preoccupied with finding faults to justify our
hatred. Our situation was aptly characterized by Jesus in
his remark, "Why do you see the speck that is in your
brother's eye, but do not notice the log that is in your own
eye?" (Matt. 7:3). More fatal than any of these moral
failings is the tyranny exercised over us by our own
egocentrism, which is the source of our moral failings. It
prevents us from finding our true selves, that "room"
Teresa of Avila said we so readily deface but do not live in.
George Eliot in her novel, *Middlemarch*, showed how
egocentrism enveloped a person so completely that it was
not even noticed until it was lifted by the near prospect of
death. She described a person who had just learned that
his illness was fatal:

> When the commonplace "We must all die,"
> transforms itself suddenly into the acute con-
> sciousness "I must die—and soon," then death
> grapples us and his fingers are cruel; after-
> wards, he may come to fold us in his arms as
> our mother did, and our last moment of earthly
> discerning may be like the first.[2]

What does such a change signify? By being brought face to face with death, people are sometimes freed of the overwhelming grip of egotism and only then realize how wonderful life can be. Perhaps this is what lay behind Paul's longing to be with Christ. He did not long for death, but fully to have a life free of anxiety, greed, discontent, pride, hatred, and a host of other evils that dominate our lives when we are still in the grip of our egotism. We do not need to await the moment of death to begin to live, but we do need to recognize how powerful are the forces that keep us in bondage and that we need God's help.

As Simone Weil points out, no matter how great our achievements may be, we can never through them attain a life that is in God's likeness, free of all evil.

> In one of Grimm's stories there is a competition between a giant and a little tailor to see which is the stronger. The giant throws a stone so high that it takes a very long time before it comes down again. The little tailor lets a bird fly and it does not come down at all.[3]

The Gospels portray Jesus as one who is able to release us from demonic possession and also from the evil that permeates our thoughts and actions. Many of us do not recognize ourselves under the general description of sinner. But if we continue to examine Jesus' effect on different people in the Gospel accounts, as we have been doing, we are likely to find out something essential about ourselves. The people in the Gospel stories are what literary critics call "figures." A figure is an individual that reveals something about other people and from whose life we can gain guidance for our own. To become like Jesus, to realize the divine image in our own lives, we are not to look at him in isolation, but at his interactions with people. We, too, need to interact with him now by seeking his help, as people did during his earthly ministry, and by obeying his teaching. We will find ourselves progressively released from the possession of evil and, as we experience our release, we shall realize how extensive our bondage is.

In the Gospel stories, there is an important difference between the way Jesus treats demons and the way he treats people. When he commands demons to leave people, they do so immediately. Yet human beings, who, in comparison with demons are puny, can ignore his commandments. Likewise, we see a contrast in his treatment of nature. He calms storms and heals diseases. But with people Jesus wants a voluntary recognition of the soundness of his teachings. The way Jesus exercised his power will now be contrasted to the way Herod and Pilate exercised theirs.

1. Trollope, Anthony. *The Warden*. New York: Dutton, 1957.

2. Eliot, George [pseud.]. *Middlemarch*. Harmsworth, UK.: Penguin Books, 1985. Actually the man's character was so hardened that he was unable to escape from the power of his egocentrism. The same was true of one character, but not another in Iris Murdoch's *The Unicorn*. Both are studied in Chapter Two of my book: *Finding Our Father*. Atlanta, GA.: John Knox Press, 1974.

3. Weil, Simone. *Waiting For God*. New York: Harper & Row, 1973: 195.

CHAPTER FOUR

A New Kind of Death

$\mathbf{M}$ atthew's Gospel begins with Jesus' genealogy. He traces it from Abraham, the first Jew, through David, Israel's greatest king, to Joseph, Jesus' father. Matthew stresses Jesus' connection with the line of David because many people in Israel believed that the Messiah or Christ would be born of the house of David. Matthew underlines the connection by reporting that in Joseph's dream the angel addressed him as "Joseph, son of David" (Matt. 1:20). No sooner has Matthew made the connection than he proceeds to break it. He tells us that Joseph was not Jesus' father because Jesus' mother, Mary, was a virgin. It would seem that Matthew should have omitted either the genealogy or the reference to the virgin birth, rather than juxtapose them at the very opening of his Gospel.

Actually, Matthew has indirectly shown us how God can achieve his purposes through people who are believers. Matthew, in contrast to Luke, devotes his attention to

Joseph. He tells us that Joseph did not seek revenge for his injury, as people who have been betrayed quite commonly do, by publicly exposing Mary's apparent infidelity. Rather, he decided to dissolve the marriage agreement quietly. But in a dream, an angel told him that Mary had not been unfaithful: the child she was carrying was the result of God's Spirit. The child was to be named Jesus, because he would save the people of Israel from their sins. When he awoke Joseph "did as the angel of the Lord commanded him; he took his wife, but knew her not until she had borne a son; and he called his name Jesus" (Matt. 1:24-5).

The philosopher in me wants to point out that Joseph was not gullible. Philosophers rightly ask for the evidence for a belief. Dreams are not considered good or adequate evidence. Therefore I feel called upon to point out that Joseph's dream should not be thought of as evidence for a belief. Rather, it is *on account of* his dream that Joseph learned what he should do and found himself with enough faith to act upon the revelation. The dream functions as a source of information and as the occasion for belief, not as evidence for the truth of what is believed. His faith was a response to a disclosure of God's intentions. Whether he acted faithfully or not was his responsibility.

Because of Joseph's faith in the power of God and faith in God's intentions to save the people of Israel, Jesus, through adoption, became a member of the house of David.

Because of Joseph's faith, people could not use the absence of a physical connection as a reason for rejecting Jesus as the Messiah. Had Joseph not adopted him, people could have used the lack of membership in the house of David as a reason to reject him. Joseph's adoption of Jesus meant that there was one less obstacle to his acceptance as the Messiah.

We can also see from this story that those of us who are not Jews are nonetheless heirs of the promises God made to the Hebrew people. We do not have to be connected to the ancient Hebrews by blood for their God to be ours, any more than Jesus had to be connected by blood to the house of David to be the Messiah. God's purposes can be, and are, achieved even when earthly connections are missing.

Joseph's reaction to the birth of Jesus was very different from that of those with political power. Immediately after the story of Joseph, Matthew describes the reaction of Herod, the King of Judea, to the birth of Jesus. Wise men from the East went to Herod's court in Jerusalem, looking for a recently born king of the Jews. Although Herod was a Jew, he held his throne under the aegis of Rome. He became deeply disturbed when the wise men told him that they had seen a star which portended the birth of a king of the Jews. Herod assumed that this king would be his rival. To answer the wise men's question, he made inquiries of the chief priests and the scribes and learned from them that the Messiah was to be born in Bethlehem. Herod told the wise men to seek the child in Bethlehem and, when they have found him, to tell him precisely where the child was, so that, he too, could worship him. Because they realized Herod's evil intentions, they did not return to Jerusalem. Herod, in a rage over their deception and in fear of a rival, had all male children aged two years and under in and around Bethlehem killed.

To Joseph the birth of Jesus meant the Messiah had come to save his people. To the wise men the birth of the Messiah was the crown and goal of their search for truth and wisdom. To Herod, who was interested in maintaining his personal power and privilege, every kind of power was a threat to his own. Just as avarice led the man in Trollope's story to interpret everything in terms of its monetary value, so, too, does political power incline those who have it to interpret everything in political terms. Avarice blinded an old man to the Christlike love of his Warden; political power blinded Herod to the glory that Joseph and the wise men saw in God's gift.

Herod also illustrates the terrible damage that political power can cause. In order to maintain his own position, he used his power to kill innocent children. The misuse of political power is always a temptation for those who have it. Its misuse on the innocent children of Bethlehem was an intimation that it would be misused on Jesus as well. Although Jesus escaped the slaughter Herod caused, he too would become an innocent victim. But ironically, it is Jesus' death which shows that the suffering of the innocent children was not in vain. Herod's misuse of power could not prevent God's purposes from being achieved and, even when the much greater political power of Rome was used to crucify Jesus, God was still able to achieve our redemption from sin and death.

Virgin births are fairly common in ancient mythology, but in the opening chapters of Matthew's Gospel there is far more than a common tale of a virgin birth. Matthew portrays for us many of the issues that the life of Jesus posed—we are brought face-to-face with them. Do we, like Joseph, in spite of bafflement about how God can work without the normal earthly connection in place, still look to God for our redemption? Are we like the wise men, seeking and finding that truth that makes sense of our lives and world? Are we like Herod, blind to everything except the power that enables us to impose our will on others and, when threatened, do we recognize brute force as the only way to make ourselves secure? At this point in time, there is not anything to be gained by trying to document Mary's virginity. Historically we simply cannot say much about it one way or the other. But that is not the way to go about the matter. Matthew has raised vital issues about the birth of Jesus *today*, just as they were raised for Joseph, the wise men, and Herod. This is true of Luke's account of the birth of Jesus as well, which adds to Matthew's the reactions of Zechariah, Elizabeth, Mary, and the shepherds to the coming of Jesus. Each of them serves as a "figure" for us to consider as we examine our own reactions to the life and teachings of Jesus.[1]

Today we have become so conscious of the misuse of power, that sometimes Christian theologians give the impression that Jesus rejected all power as evil. But it is clear that he did not dismiss it as illegitimate. For example, when asked by those who sought to trap him into an indiscretion whether taxes should be paid to Caesar, he asked them for a coin," 'Whose likeness and inscription is this?' They said, 'Caesar's.' Then he said to them, 'Render therefore to Caesar the things that are Caesar's, and to God the things that are God's'" (Matt. 22:20-21). He left it up to his followers to determine the balance between our obligations to our earthly rulers and our obligations to God. This forces us to learn the value and limits of the proper exercise of power. But his statement clearly implies that there is such a thing as the legitimate exercise of power by earthly rulers, and that this is limited because of God's reality.

Pilate, the Roman governor (or procurator, since Judea was not significant enough to be a province), was not as wanton as Herod in his use of power. After Jesus' arrest, the Jewish leaders brought him before Pilate because they did not have the power to put him to death. In his examination, Pilate asked Jesus bluntly,

"Are you the king of the Jews?" Jesus said,

"Is that your own idea, or have others suggested it to you?" "What! am I a Jew?," said Pilate. "Your own nation and their chief priests have brought you before me. What have you done?" Jesus replied, "My kingdom does not belong to this world. If it did, my followers would be fighting to save me from arrest by the Jews. My kingly authority comes from elsewhere." "You are a king, then?" said Pilate. "'King' is your word. My task is to bear witness to the truth. For this I was born; for this I came into the world, and all who are not deaf to the truth listen to my voice." Pilate said, "What is truth?", and with those words went out again to the Jews. "For my part," he said, "I find no case against him" (John 18:34-8, NEB).

Pilate, unlike Herod, did not find the possibility that Jesus was king of the Jews threatening, probably because Jesus made it clear that his kingdom was not one based on force. But he was also not concerned with Jesus' claim that his teachings were a witness to the truth and that those who were not deaf to the claims of truth would listen to him. Pilate easily turned aside Jesus' claim with the rhetorical question, "What is truth?" Pilate expected no answer because he was sophisticated enough to know that philosophers and religious leaders had never been able to agree on the big questions of life. As an active, practical person Pilate simply dismissed such questions from serious consideration. For him, as for so many in our culture today, the search for truth was significant only for its practical results, in such areas as economic development, medical advances, and military power.

However, Pilate did care about justice, and wanted to release Jesus because no case had been made against him. But he ran into a problem that those who have power cannot avoid. People, in fact, have different convictions about what we ought to do, what we can hope for, and what is true. Conflicts occur between them, just as they did between the Jewish leaders and Jesus. Whether they like it or not, those with power are drawn into these conflicts. The Jews, who disagreed with Jesus, wanted Pilate to do something about their disagreement.

This put Pilate in a bind. He himself had no confidence in anyone's ability to resolve the big questions of life, but as procurator, he must keep the peace. Since there was danger that their controversy would lead to serious public disorder, he sacrificed his desire to be just so as to maintain public order. Ironically, it was not because of Herod's cruel use of power, but because of Pilate's reluctant decision that Jesus suffered execution.

Those with responsibility for maintenance of the peace, even if they care about justice, as Pilate did, are under pressure to sacrifice justice in the face of a threat to public order. In spite of the faith of eighteenth and nineteenth century political reformers, such as Voltaire and Marx, in the "verdict of history," the arena of political decisions is not likely to be a place where the big issues of life are decided solely; or even primarily, on the basis of truth and justice.

Pilate ritually and publicly washed his hands to indicate his personal disagreement with the charges against Jesus and made it clear that the issues in the controversy had not been settled. His enemies succeeded in having Jesus condemned to death, but not without it being made clear that what they were doing was unjust and it did not settle the matter of who was right. Ironically, Pilate, who initially had tried to pass over the big issues of life, made it clear that Jesus was executed because of what he taught and that in spite of the sentence he passed on Jesus the question still remained, Is what he teaches true? Pilate, who was not a Jew and something of a cynic, because he was concerned to be just, allowed the question of the truth of what Jesus taught to remain in the forefront. In all the confusion of arrest, accusations, the smell, dust, heat, and noise of the crowd, it did not get lost. Jesus' refusal to resist arrest and his refusal to have his disciples fight to save him enabled Pilate to realize that the truth of Jesus' teachings was truly the issue between him and his accusers. Jesus' behavior did not allow the threat of a cruel death by crucifixion deflect the focus of attention.

Jesus, then, was a particular kind of victim of injustice. To keep the issue in the forefront by a commitment to truth was an active, not a passive, role. Because Jesus' death is so familiar, this feature of his death is easily missed. To highlight it, we will briefly examine the death of Socrates, which is not as familiar.

At his trial, Socrates was accused of three things: atheism, leading young people astray (no doubt, Alcibiades was especially in mind), and endangering the security of Athens. Those who brought the charges demanded the death penalty. This punishment was ridiculously severe. The jury of five hundred citizens would have been happy to close the whole affair with a minor fine. According to Athenian law, the jury had to choose between the alternatives proposed by the plaintiff and the defendant. Socrates' friends begged him to propose a fine, and even offered to pay it for him. But Socrates refused. He had obeyed a divine call to awaken his city to its ignorance and its need to search for a truer way to live. He said that he was of course only a minor person in the great city of Athens, no more than a gadfly, stinging a large beast in order to make it take notice of the way it was stumbling along, heedless of its direction. To carry out this mission, he had neglected his own business affairs. Now, as an old man, he was poor. He therefore proposed that the city provide him with a pension in recognition of his services.

The jury had to decide between the death penalty and a pension for services. The majority were so outraged with Socrates for making the situation so awkward that they voted for the death penalty. Everyone expected that, while in prison, Socrates would come to his senses and admit that he was wrong. The city officials tried to arrange for Socrates to escape, but he refused to cooperate: Either I have been a benefactor and should receive a pension, or my accusers are right.

The jury had not reckoned on the seriousness of this little citizen; it was amazed at his passionate love of truth and at his deep commitment to the well-being of his fellow citizens. By his refusal to back down, even in the face of death, Socrates forced his fellow citizens to face a vital issue. Is the basis of life to go unexamined? Are we just to stumble along? Will the gods allow this to go unpunished? If he had accepted a minor fine, or, when he saw that they meant business, escaped from prison, people would have been able to slide over these questions and continue to live untroubled, but superficial, lives.

By accepting a grossly unjust death, Socrates allowed the people of his city to continue to live the way they wanted to, but only at the price of the death of a wise, generous citizen, who had devoted his life to their betterment. To be this kind of victim is not something that just happens. Socrates' and Jesus' deaths differed from those of countless victims of injustice because of the way they conducted themselves. Each of them suffered from injustice in such a way that they caused people to face the big questions of life.

There is, however, a very great difference between their deaths. The people who executed Socrates could see quite clearly what they were doing: killing a person who claimed to be their benefactor. What made it so awful was that the only harm that Socrates had done was to annoy people by his persistent questioning, which for most of them amounted to little more than being a tiresome nuisance. He posed no public danger. It is shameful to injure small people precisely because they can do so little harm. But by his integrity, this little person made the Athenians aware that what they were doing was inexcusably shameful.

With Jesus it is very different. The difference was voiced in the very first words he uttered from the cross: "Father, forgive them, for they know not what they do" (Luke 23:34). Jesus had conducted himself in such a way that the issue, Is what I teach true? would not be lost. That he had sought to be his people's benefactor—healing the sick, casting out demons, welcoming outcasts, lifting the burden of a misconceived law—was plainly before all those who had eyes to see and ears to hear. Pilate openly stated that Jesus had done nothing to deserve execution. But the magnitude of their deed was mercifully not plain to them. The full horror of crucifying the Son of the Most High was not plainly seen by the people who demanded and those who carried out the execution.

This is known from Jesus' own words. Jesus asked his Father to forgive them because they were ignorant of the full significance of their action. They were spared a full knowledge because it would have been an impossible burden for anyone to bear. Some were simply onlookers at a public execution, a rather common sight in those days. Many of those who knew that Pilate said Jesus was innocent might well have thought, as we today sometimes do in the face of a tragedy, "What a shame! It is really too bad, but that sort of thing does happen." The religious officials had the duty to protect the holy law entrusted to them. Apparently some of them were very much in favor of his execution; but perhaps others regretted it but believed that it had to be done because Jesus simply could not be allowed to get away with what he was saying. On and on we could go with our speculation about the motives and feelings of various people on that awful day, but whatever their motives and feelings may have been, Jesus did not believe that any of them knew precisely what they were doing.

When we are being treated unfairly and another person does not realize how awful what they are doing to us actually is, we want to scream, "Stop it! Can't you see how terrible it is!" But Jesus did not. He did not want people to perceive the full horror of what they were doing. His very first words in his agony on the cross were not even addressed to those who were treating him so unjustly. His first words were addressed to his Father, and were on their behalf, not his own. He thus made it clear to them and to us that he willingly accepted what happened to him without hatred or scorn.

Because of his behavior we today can perceive the greatness of his death. He died so that we might live, showing us that God's response to our failure to live as we ought is not rejection, not abandonment, not extermination, but is a love that endures the evil we do to others, to ourselves, and to God. We see that God became a human being in order to suffer *as we*, who are creatures, suffer, and through that suffering to give us access to *zoe*, the uncreated life of

God. Only those who see in Jesus the love of God incarnate can bear to look fully and openly at what they do to others and to themselves, without being overcome with self-hatred. Because of who he is and what he has done, we find in that terrible death the inspiration to live.

Let us now turn our attention to the two thieves who were crucified with Jesus. They were faced with a clear choice, and it is the same choice with which we are faced. We have been looking at various people with whom Jesus dealt as figures. Some people, like Mary Magdalene, have lost control of their lives; others, like Nicodemus, do not understand what Jesus is talking about; still others, like the rich young man, are kept from following Jesus because of their possessions. But *all* of us are like the thieves who were crucified with Jesus.

A thief is someone who has taken what is not his or hers as their own. We are like thieves because we have sought to steal ourselves, robbing God of our lives. We take it for granted that we belong to ourselves. No one owns us. We resist, and rightly resist, infringement on our life, liberty, and property. We insist on our right to do what we like as long as it makes us happy. Nonetheless, we are thieves because we hold onto ourselves as if we owned ourselves and may do with ourselves as we wish. Even if we happen to like going to church, we still feel that our minds, wills, and bodies are our own, and no one else's—not even God's. From God's point of view each of us is significant and irreplaceable, bearing the image of God, but we are also thieves because we owe our lives to our maker and sustainer. As it is put in Psalm 49:7, "Truly no man can ransom himself, or give to God the price of his life. . ."

That we are thieves, robbing God of ourselves, is made graphically apparent in the lives of the two unfortunate wretches that hung on crosses next to Jesus. They were stripped of all that they had—no possessions remained. All that was left was their very lives, and those were steadily and inexorably passing away with each drop of blood. All that was left was themselves, and even that was now going. Soon there would be nothing left at all. Their plight ought to make us aware of how inaccurate our attitude toward ourselves is. The fact that no other human being owns us, does not mean we belong to ourselves. Death makes that clear.

There was no question in the minds of those people who witnessed their crucifixion that these men were thieves. The only question about them was what kind of thief—a repentant or an unrepentant one? The thief who refused to repent accepted the fact that he was a thief. He had lived like one and would die like one. He was a perfectly well adjusted human being: What others thought of him and what he thought of himself were in perfect agreement. But he did not include in his life God's estimate of him. Rather, he cursed an innocent man who told people that whoever seeks to keep his or her life, shall lose it.

The thief who repented was also well adjusted. People said he was a thief and he knew he was a thief. But he became realistic. He came to recognize that his greatest crime was committed against his maker. Therefore he did not curse Jesus; he recognized that Jesus was not a thief, but belonged to God. He wanted to join Jesus, to be part of the kingdom to which he belonged, apparently without knowing what it was, except that to rob other people and to rob God was the way of death.

Not all of us have stolen from others, but we do think that we belong to ourselves. There is no question but that this is to be a thief in the sight of God. The question is which kind of thief are we: a repentant or an unrepentant one? May we learn to pray, as did Dostoevsky, one of the world's greatest literary artists, "Like a thief, receive me Lord." It is only as repentant thieves that we shall ever hear the words that Jesus spoke to that great-hearted man who turned to him on the cross, "Today you will be with me in Paradise" (Luke 23:43).

What did Jesus mean? Jesus apparently did not enter Paradise until his resurrection. It is possible that Jesus used the word "paradise" to allude to the condition of innocence which Adam and Eve enjoyed before they refused to obey God. That very day, the repentant thief is assured, he will be restored to the prefallen state of innocence in which one willingly belongs to God.

Jesus was next concerned about his mother, who stood near the cross with her sister, along with Mary Magdalene and one of the disciples. Jesus said to his mother, "'Woman, behold, your son!' Then he said to the disciple, 'Behold, your mother!' And from that hour the disciple took her to his own home" (John 19:26-7). His words show that it is a false spirituality that excludes concern for the earthly welfare of people, and obligations to family members. They also suggest that even though Jesus would be at the right hand of the Father, he wanted his mother to receive the care that can be supplied only by one who is in this world. He therefore entrusted the care of his mother to a disciple whom he loved, not only as a disciple, but as a friend.

Jesus' first three concerns as he was dying were all for others: those who had crucified him, the two thieves who suffered alongside him, his mother. But suddenly he was overcome and cried out in a loud voice, "My God, My God, why hast thou forsaken me?" (Mark 15:34).

Although Jesus had always directed his life toward God, he had begun to experience the effects of a disobedient life. *Zoe*, the uncreated life of God, which he had enjoyed and sought to share with others, was being withdrawn. For some time he had realized that he was to be crucified. As horrible as that was, he had apparently come to terms with it. It was only in the garden of Gethsemane, on the night in which he was arrested, that he realized that he might have to endure it while the presence of God's life was being withdrawn. His disciples reported that he sweat great drops like blood, as he prayed, "Father, if thou art willing, remove this cup from me; nevertheless, not my will, but thine, be done" (Luke 23:42). On the cross, what he had dreaded began to happen, and he voiced his distress in the words of Psalm 22:1. From Jesus' distress, we learn how far he was willing to go for our sake. However much he dreaded it, he was willing to experience the full consequences of our having become thieves. Ironically, the only one who fully yielded himself to God is the one who experienced what those who have sought to possess their lives ought to experience: the absence of God's loving presence.

After having endured those awful moments, Jesus spoke the most simple words: "I thirst" (John 19:28). These words are perfectly natural since he had lost so much fluid from sweating and bleeding. They are not profound. Yet they are among the most awesome words ever uttered. The Word of God, spoken at creation—"Let there be light. ... let there be a firmament in the midst of the waters....let the waters bring forth swarms of living creatures.... let us make man in our image. ... (Gen. 1:1ff.)—became incarnate (John 1:1-18), and said, "I thirst."

As we mentioned earlier, in "East Coker," T.S. Eliot contrasted two beginnings. If we are only earthly creatures, our end is the very earth from which human beings have evolved. But if our beginning is the Word of God that not only formed the earth and us from the earth, but enables us to receive the Spirit of God, then our end is to share in the uncreated life of God. Our end is either the earth or to receive the Word of God and live.

We today find it difficult to hear the Word of God, largely because of a misunderstanding. It is widely assumed that the Jewish people in their innocence, composed an artless tale about a voice that magically called the members of the universe into existence. We, more sober people, no longer in the infancy of the human race, know better. Science gives us the answer.

But in fact, science does not even treat the question of the ultimate basis of the universe. Given the existence of the universe, science can answer many questions about its operations. But from a study of its operations, we cannot tell why there is a universe at all. The ultimate basis of the universe is beyond the power of science to determine. Its existence is taken as the starting point for science.

Belief in God among the ancient Hebrews did not arise because they were engaged in speculation about the ultimate basis of the universe. It arose because Abraham was addressed by God. God took the initiative, and Abraham believed the Word of God that established a covenant with him and his promised descendants. That is how belief in God started among the ancient Hebrews. Only later did the people of Israel begin to realize that the God with whom they were dealing was not only their God, but the God of all people and the Lord of the natural world. The natural world is not independent of God but is dependent on God's Word for its order and being because God is *El Shaddai*, the almighty or the all-sufficient that lacks nothing, but who graciously creates a people and promises to be a benefactor to them, and through them, to all people.[2]

The status of the universe as the highest and best reality had never been called into question by the ancient Babylonians, Egyptians, or Greeks. All the so-called creation stories assumed that the divine and earthly realms were parts of the same universe, and that gods and human beings were merely members of different divisions of the same whole. The Hindus, who call the status of the universe into question by comparing the universe to a divine dream, do not make precise demarkation of the universe from its source in the fashion of the ancient Hebrews. Because the ancient Hebrews' God was *El Shaddai*, they came to realize that unlike the universe which is dependent on God, God is utterly independent of the existence of the universe.[3] God is utterly self-sufficient, and the existence of a universe at every moment of time (not just at the beginning of the universe) depends on the power of God's Word. Genesis 1 is based on a Babylonian myth. It is primarily the feature of divine self-sufficiency that transformed the ancient Babylonian story of creation into the ancient Hebrews' novel conviction about the status of the natural world. This new and profound conviction was expressed in a simple story about a voice that calls things into existence.

Once we *understand* the relation of *El Shaddai* to the universe, whether or not we *accept* the ancient Hebrew conviction that the universe depends on the Word of God for its existence and preservation largely turns upon our ability to recognize Jesus as the Word of God incarnate. All too often we divide Jesus' life into that which is divine and that which is human. When he spoke sublimely we take it that the divine part of him was shining forth. When he became angry and cast the money changers from the Temple, we take it that the human part of him was uppermost. We find it difficult to recognize that whatever he did or said was human, because the Word of God became a human being, and whatever he did or said was divine, even the most simple, natural human words that you and I can say, such as "I thirst."

The words, "I thirst," show us that to be incarnate means that the Word of God, on which the universe depends, itself became dependent. But unlike us, who have resisted God's will by holding on to ourselves like robbers, Jesus realized our destiny because he did not resist the divine will. The Word of God incarnate, though like us in so far as it was dependent on such things as water to live, was also different from every other human being because the Word of God incarnate was the Son of Man.

Biblical scholars are confident that Jesus referred to himself as the Son of Man. It puzzled his hearers. In Hebrew it means "Son of Adam," since "adam" means "man" in Hebrew. It implies that what Adam, the first man, failed to achieve, *bar adam*, the second man, accomplished. We all have failed to achieve the intentions of God, and have violated the principle *arche* of our being. Sometimes our resistance takes the form of misunderstanding, as when, for example, we set aside the creation of Genesis 1 as a mere myth of a naive people. We resist the Word of God when it became incarnate by saying such things as, "After all, Jesus was a man, and we can only partly reconstruct his life story as it took place." Although this is true, it should not keep us from also seeing him as the man who lived up to God's intentions. We resist doing so because it would mean that we must change the way we live and learn from him how we are to live.

Just as we frequently misrepresent the creation story as the artless product of a prescientific people, we hear Jesus' words, "I thirst," as nothing more than something that you and I might say. They are indeed words that you or I might say, but they are also words that God said. This is indeed the awesomeness of the Gospel stories. He who is without beginning and end, he who is almighty—the *El Shaddai* who needs nothing to be full, complete, and glorious for ever and ever—degraded himself when the Word of God became a human being; for to move from a higher to a lower grade of being, is degrading. But the incarnation is much more degrading than for you or I to become, for example, a dog, because the Word of creation became a creature. The source of the universe, became a member of the universe. That is what the Word of God did solely and wholly for our sakes. Laughing and smiling, sweating and smelling, teaching and healing, loving and judging, calling and weeping, bleeding and calling out, "I thirst," the Word of God acted and spoke.

How could God so degrade himself? We cannot be worth such a price. We do not take ourselves that seriously. But this is the cardinal sin, the original sin, the sin of selling ourselves short. We just cannot believe that we matter all that much. By selling ourselves short, we sell God short. We deny the greatness of God's purpose and the greatness of his love. When we are told that Jesus said, "I thirst," we do not hear in these words the Word of God, and tremble at the seriousness with which God takes us. The Word of God became the *bar adam*, the Son of Man, that we might hear in the voice of a human being the voice of God.

When Jesus was born another name of God was revealed: Immanuel, God with us (Matt. 1:23). Why did God choose to be with us in this way? Could not God simply have forgiven us without becoming incarnate? He could have, but he didn't. By becoming "Immanuel" he has shown us how he removes evil.

Evil causes suffering. You cannot be exposed to hatred, jealousy, conceit, cruelty, or other forms of evil without suffering from their effects. God is aware of the evil we do.

It causes him to suffer because he cares about our welfare.[4] There is a sense in which God does not suffer. But he suffers only from afar, so to speak. To put it more precisely, he suffers as the Creator suffers, not as creatures such as we suffer. God became Immanuel in Jesus Christ in order to live as a creature lives, subject to all the physical wear and tear that creatures are subject to, and also subject to the effects of evil as human beings are. God became Immanuel, God with us, to suffer as a human being suffers.

Something of the greatness of this act can be appreciated by a comparison with Dostoevsky's novel, *Crime and Punishment*. A young man named Raskolnikov killed an old woman, ostensibly to steal a few coins. But in fact he wished to assert his superiority. It was as though he stood on a height above other people, with nothing on the horizon to limit or restrict him. He believed that right and wrong were conventions legitimate for ordinary people, but not binding on superior people—the "Napoleons" of the world. He deliberately transgressed a forbidden boundary, killing a person, to prove that he was one of those superior people.

He then began to experience the consequences of his outlook and crime. He was indeed alone and had to live out of his own resources, without being replenished or affirmed by contact with anyone. God, in contrast to us, can live on high alone, above all creation, because he has the resources within himself to live and live well. But we do not. God allowed Raskolnikov to have what he wanted: to be alone. This is why he began to feel the agony of being unable to be close to anyone, and to realize that he was now permanently cut off by his transgression.

There was one exception. Sonya, a prostitute who was forced to live as she did to help her destitute parents, was the only person who could penetrate his utter isolation. Her love enabled him to confess his crime and accept the justice of his punishment by a court of law. Together they went into exile. Raskolnikov explained that Sonya was able to penetrate his isolation because she too had killed. She had not killed another person, but had "killed" herself by sacrificing herself as a prostitute for the sake of her starving family. Because she had "killed," she was bonded to him, and thus able to penetrate his isolation, and ultimately to lead him to his redemption from his crime and the utter isolation that was its consequence. We have the paradox that a criminal, one who has killed, has a vital connection to a victim, one who has been killed. Although the guilty and defiled and the innocent and pure are opposites, their suffering has a established a deep and life-giving bond.

Dostoevsky has given us an insight into how God redeems us through the sacrifice of Jesus. It is not enough for God, who loves us, to suffer because we injure ourselves and one another. Nor is God satisfied to give us understanding of the consequences of our actions, and to guide us through the goodness of the created order (as we illustrated in our discussion of the connection between religion and art), and to call us through holy people over the ages in every land. God was not content to stay at a distance. God became a human being in order to suffer *as we suffer*. The Word of God incarnate in all purity went as far from God's ways as we ourselves have strayed. He became an outcast from the mainstream of society so that he would have a vital connection with outcasts. He became condemned as a criminal and died among thieves so that he would have a bond with criminals. He became an innocent victim so that he would be identified with those who suffer unjustly. He was forsaken by all his friends and companions so that he was united to those who are forsaken. He became utterly vulnerable to be like those who have no one to help them. Only when he had fully achieved his identification with us on the cross, did he say, "It is finished" (John 19:30). He endured every kind of distress so that human beings could no longer say, "God is not in this place; there is no help for me." He suffered, not that we might not suffer, but so that God's suffering may be like ours. He is indeed Immanuel, God with us.

Christ by his passion not only forged a vital bond between our suffering and God's suffering, but he also revealed that his followers, like everyone else, would be vulnerable to natural processes. Jesus himself experienced hunger, fatigue, aging, and death. We are to reduce and relieve the suffering that is the result of our being human beings as much as possible, as we learn from Jesus' ministry and teachings. But no matter what we do, some of this kind of suffering is the inevitable consequence of being alive as a physical human being with *bios*, biological or natural life, that finally runs out. However fortunate in this life, everyone will eventually die, just as the people Jesus healed or raised from the dead eventually died.

We dread the passage of time because it reminds us that we are subject to aging, illness, and death. Even if we are religious, we frequently wonder why God does not arrange things better so that we and those we love do not have to suffer so much. Isn't God love? Isn't God redeemer? Isn't God savior? Why does he not save us and those we love from all our suffering? Shouldn't things be better arranged to take account of our interests, needs, desires, hopes, and aspirations?

By facing our vulnerability as natural beings we can root out the incorrect idea that if we pray and obey Jesus,

God will always protect us from natural harm. Clearly, Jesus who always obeyed God, suffered from natural processes. This vulnerability is not a punishment that results from the disobedience of Adam and Eve. Nature did not "fall" with human disobedience, so that its operation changed from being always benign to causing us injury at times as a punishment. We certainly can cause injury to ourselves through natural processes, such as through overeating, but this is not because nature's law has been changed to punish gluttony. We know this because the natural laws in operation before and after the existence of human beings are the same. Human beings have existed only a few million years, and the same natural processes have been operative for several billion years.[5]

Christ's passion also revealed a division between two categories of suffering. A great deal of suffering springs from selfishness, ruthless ambitions, envy, greed, the desire to be superior to others, and other misuses of our freedom. We move so easily from a moment of contentment to misery merely by hearing about the achievement of our contemporaries. Reading the class letters in an alumni/ae magazine is usually enough to stir up a host of resentments and regrets. Because our self-preoccupation, every day, and nearly every hour, is marked with suffering.

Christ came to save us from the suffering that is avoidable and the consequence of our own sin. He made this possible by showing that suffering is of two kinds. One category includes all the suffering that is the result of our egocentrism, for example, suffering caused by ambition, greed, and envy that leads to self-inflicted suffering and also to actions that injure other people. The other category is innocent suffering. It includes the suffering we undergo as a result of other people's actions, and the suffering that results from natural causes. As long as people do not use their freedom according to God's ways, people will injure one another by their unjust acts. Because Jesus was utterly free of all envy, self-seeking ambition, and hatred, he never acted unjustly and never suffered from self-inflicted injury. Whatever he suffered was suffered in complete innocence. His suffering was caused either by people's injustices or by natural processes. His life opens our eyes to the possibility that all our suffering may become like his, wholly innocent suffering. Because of Jesus, we can seek to be just to others always, and to suffer only as the result of injustices committed by others and the effects of natural processes. To follow Christ is to *desire* to become like him and to *strive* to become like him. The more a Christian succeeds in becoming like Christ, the less suffering he or she inflicts on self and others. We can also become more like Christ by learning from the injustices we suffer. Our pain can teach us how horrible injustice is, and strengthen our efforts to work for justice, and to be forgiven for the injustices we ourselves have committed.

We must also learn to accept the inevitability of suffering because we are natural beings, subject to the wear and tear of nature's working. We are to do whatever we can to prevent and relieve such suffering but we are to recognize that whatever we cannot avoid or relieve is part of what it is to be a physical being. In other words, we have to face the truth that we are natural beings, free of the illusions caused by our egocentric perspective.

We can accept our own innocent suffering only as Jesus accepted his in the garden of Gethsemane: with dread—that is, with the desire that it not happen—and yet trusting in God. With fear and trembling, we are to desire that all our suffering be the result only of the inevitable consequences of being a creature, rooted in the workings of the natural world, and that none of our suffering be self-inflicted or the result of our own injustices. With trust in our Father's power to redeem all creatures from unrighteousness and death, we bear what we cannot change at a particular instant of time. When Jesus had done all he could do, his innocence and trust enabled him to say, "Father, into thy hands I commit my spirit!" (Luke 23:46). May we, when we have done all that we can do, also offer ourselves into God's care. If we seek to follow Christ—to allow our suffering to become like his: free of self-seeking and malice—then it will cease to be pointless suffering. It will be like his own: innocent and borne for the sake of God's redemption of the world.

Life under God is strenuous, but not grim. We have the power to improve things; we may enjoy the beauty of the world; we are to enjoy the glories of life; and we have Christ, our blessed Lord. Without him we should simply suffer and not have the hope that our suffering may become like his.

1. For a discussion of Mary's reaction, see Chapter Four in my book: *Temptation*. Cambridge, MA.: Cowley Publications, 1986.

2. For more information of the importance of the name *El Shaddai* see: Lockyer, Herbert. *All the Divine Names and Titles in the Bible*. Grand Rapids, MI: Zondervan, 1975.

3. See: Sokolowski, Robert. *The God of Faith and Reason*. Notre Dame, IN.: Notre Dame Univ. Press, 1982.

4. There is a sense in which God does not suffer. Technically it is expressed by saying that God does not suffer in God's essence. To suffer is to be acted upon, or to be passive in relation to something else. But something besides God exists only by God's creative action at every instant of time. Everything is passive in relation to God's creative action. There is nothing to affect God prior to and apart from God's primal creative activity. Our very power to disobey God's will, and thus cause God to suffer, is possible only by God's creative action. God freely chooses to expose himself to suffering by interacting with creatures: as Creator, aware of all that occurs, and as incarnate redeemer, interacting with creatures as a human being.

5. For a fuller discussion of our vulnerability to natural processes see my: *Traces of God in a Frequently Hostile World*. Cambridge, MA.: Cowley Publications, 1981.

CHAPTER FIVE

Transfiguration

The innermost part of the ancient Jewish Temple was the Holy of Holies, which only the High Priest was permitted to enter. In 70 A.D. when the Jews rebelled against Roman rule, Roman soldiers thrust aside fierce resistance and entered the Holy of Holies. As in 169 B.C. when the Temple was plundered of gold and silver in a raid by Antiochus, there were no statues representing the divine being the Jews worshipped. This fed the rumor throughout the Mediterranean world that the Jews were atheists. The Romans were unable to understand the Jewish conviction that God cannot be represented by anything we can make, and that this conviction is best symbolized by the *absence* of sensible representations.[1]

According to the Bible, for God's nature and intentions to be known at all, God must take the initiative and reveal them. He has done it in various ways. He revealed himself to Moses through a voice from a burning bush that was not consumed, to Isaiah in a vision in the Temple, to Joseph in a dream. Often he has revealed his purposes through the inspired speech and writing of prophets. He has also revealed himself through names, such as *El Shaddai* and Yahweh.

In the Incarnation, he revealed a new name: Immanuel, God with us. This revelation was as far removed from the predominant ancient Jewish way of understanding God as was the emptiness of the Holy of Holies from the Roman way of understanding their gods. The Jews had no room within their understanding to accommodate an incarnation. The Jewish frame of reference could accept the possibility that Jesus was the Son of Man. People were confused by Jesus' use of the expression, largely because it had fallen out of currency. The claim that Jesus was a human being, and the only human being that had fully achieved God's intentions, was audacious but not unthinkable within the ancient Jewish religion. But to call him "Immanuel," God with us, meaning that God had become incarnate, was clearly not acceptable. Yet, according to biblical scholars, immediately after his resurrection, his followers said "Jesus is Lord," using a title hitherto reserved for God alone.

The God of Israel had a distinctive name, Yahweh, meaning "he who causes to be." This name was never pronounced, because of the awesome reverence attached to it. By the tenth century before Christ, 'Adonai, the Hebrew word for "Lord," was used as a substitute for Yahweh, and not long after that, was regularly used in place of Yahweh. The ancient Jews understood 'Adonai to mean the Lord of creation and the Holy One of Israel. The earliest Christian creed, "Jesus is Lord," made it clear that Jesus was Immanuel, God with us. Within the understanding of ancient Judaism, it was unthinkable that *anything* could be identified with God. Yet that is precisely what Jesus' first followers, most of whom were Jews, were driven to claim of Jesus. The fact that the Incarnation is unthinkable within the framework of the ancient Jewish religion makes the conviction all the more remarkable. Jesus is not just a teacher or a victim of injustice, but he is Lord.

The Greek philosophers, and those who read them, had a far more sophisticated outlook than those who believed in the gods and goddesses of mythology. For these thinkers the ultimate reality was comprised of impersonal forces and principles. This is similar to modern science, which regards the world as governed by impersonal laws and principles. The notion of the ultimate reality being a person, born of a woman, working as a carpenter, dying on a cross, seemed to be a reversion to the unsophisticated mythology of gods and goddesses. This was why Paul said that the Gospel was foolishness to the Greeks, meaning those who had been shaped by the ancient Greek philosophic outlook.

But in reality the beliefs of the Jews were more profound than even the philosophically sophisticated Romans and Greeks. For in the last analysis, the impersonal forces and principles of the philosophers were parts of the universe, not its source. For the Jew, God was *El Shaddai*, the Almighty, and did not share the universe with anything or anyone, but was its all-sufficient source. Nothing could represent, much less be identified with, God. Yet Jesus' first followers, for the most part Jews, claimed that Jesus was Lord, uniting in his one person two disparate realities.

His followers agreed with those Jews who did not follow Jesus when they acknowledged that we cannot *comprehend* the Incarnation. Our minds can at best only understand created realities, and even in this domain, there is much we have been unable to comprehend. It is not surprising that the way in which God became incarnate exceeds our comprehension. But we can recognize that the Incarnation is true, just as we can recognize that a person is a human being even though we do not yet know the essence of human nature.

We can recognize that Jesus is God incarnate through his actions. I do not mean that Jesus' miracles prove that Jesus is God incarnate. His extraordinary power to perform wonders, as they are called in the New Testament, exhibits or reveals the *extent* of his authority. Until he acted no one could know how far it extended, as we see reflected in the remark, "even wind and sea obey him" (Mark 4:4). His disciples knew that he had power over demons before he stilled the waters, but did not know that he had power to control storms as well. But such acts did not establish that Jesus was God incarnate. In Jesus' day, anyone with extraordinary power was thought to have received it either from God or from Satan. At most Jesus' extraordinary power to perform wonders would show that he was *from* God, not that he was God incarnate. (Jesus' opponents said he was from Satan).

There was one act, however, that only God could perform: the forgiveness of sin. God and God alone had the power to forgive disobedience. This was frequently the focus of the controversy between Jesus and the Pharisees. For example, when a Pharisee invited Jesus to a meal a notorious prostitute managed to get into the house and, standing behind Jesus, wet his feet with her tears and then wiped them with her hair. She kissed his feet and anointed them. In effect, she did what the Pharisee ought to have done for an honored guest. (It was the custom for the host to greet a guest with a kiss after a servant had washed and anointed the guest's feet).

When the Pharisee saw what the woman was doing, he was scandalized. He thought to himself, this man is not a prophet. If he were, he would have realized what sort of woman was touching and defiling him. Jesus was aware of the Pharisee's disapproval. So he asked him,

> 'Simon, I have something to say to you . . . .
> A certain creditor had two debtors; one owed
> five hundred denarii, and the other fifty.
> When they could not pay, he forgave them
> both. Now which of them will love him
> more?' Simon answered, 'The one, I sup-
> pose, to whom he forgave more.' And he
> said to him, 'You have judged rightly. . . .
> Therefore I tell you, her sins, which are
> many, are forgiven, for she loved much; but
> he who is forgiven little, loves little.' And he
> said to her, 'Your sins are forgiven '(Luke
> 7:40-4 and 47-8).

This deeply offended the Pharisee and his guests. They asked, "Who is this, who even forgives sins?" (Luke 7:49).

Jesus' assumption of the prerogative of God and the offense it caused was also explicit when he told a man suffering from paralysis that his sins were forgiven: "And the scribes and Pharisees began to question, saying, 'Who is this that speaks blasphemies? Who can forgive sins but God only?'" (Luke 5:21).

This may appear to be no more than a family squabble. Why should we take it seriously? It is clear that Jesus realized that the forgiveness of God, which he was author-ized to grant, may have meant no more to some people than pearls do to swine. For example, he told a parable about a servant who owed such an immense debt to his lord that he could not repay it. He and his family were to be sold into slavery, as was the custom. He begged to be allowed more time, and he would repay it all. Out of pity his lord remitted the entire debt. But the magnanimity of the deed did not affect the man. As he went out of his master's house, he met a fellow servant who owed him a relatively small amount of money and demanded immediate payment. He refused the plea for more time and had the man arrested. When his lord heard about his behavior, he summoned him and said,

> 'You wicked servant! I forgave you all that debt because you besought me; and should not you have had mercy on your fellow servant, as I had mercy on you?' And in anger his lord delivered him to the jailers, till he should pay all his debt. So also my heavenly Father will do to every one of you, if you do not forgive your brother from your heart (Matt. 18:33-5).

Jesus was teaching us that to *receive* forgiveness is not simply to have our debts or trespasses remitted. It requires us to want to become like the one who forgives us. In the act of accepting the generosity of his lord, the man incurred the obligation to be generous to others. He should have wanted to become a person who could act as did his lord. Even though he had been forgiven an immense debt, he was not filled with gratitude, as was the prostitute who had washed Jesus' feet and wiped them with her hair. The prostitute knew that without forgiveness and help from God she could not rise above what she had become, any more than could Mary Magdalene, tax collectors, and those who were defiled. The man in the parable knew that he was hopelessly in debt. Only his lord's mercy could keep him and his family from slavery. But he did not recognize that the reception of the generosity that saves us must lead us at least to want to be changed so that we will treat others generously. Even though God in his mercy seeks to forgive, we must actually receive the uncreated life of God, *zoe*, that begins our transformation into the divine likeness, enabling us to forgive just as we have been forgiven. In the parable, the man was put into prison until he should pay all his debt. It was clear that he could never do it. From the application of the parable to his hearers—that they would be imprisoned unless they learned to forgive—we realize that the intention of punishing the man was to help change his heart. The threat of punishment or punishment itself sometimes enables us to see the seriousness of what we have done or failed to do, and when we see it, we sometimes desire to become a better person.[2]

Today many people think that love and punishment are contradictory. But if they were, then not only would Christianity fail to make sense, but life itself would become unbearable. The connection between love and punishment is portrayed in Milan Kundera's unusual novel, *The Unbearable Lightness of Being*.[3]

Kundera describes two ways to view our actions. On one view our actions are utterly transient. In a philosophical meditation that serves as a prelude to the story, Kundera symbolizes the transiency of our actions by sexual promiscuity. He tells us that a body loved with fidelity affects the soul because fidelity affirms the uniqueness of the person that is loved. Promiscuous lovemaking intends to be transitory, that is, it intends to avoid personal involvement and to be free of consequences. The more it realizes this intention, the less "weight" (or significance) the sexual act has beyond momentary pleasure.

The main character in the novel is a physician who is

utterly promiscuous. There is no emotional involvement between him and those with whom he sleeps. Their actions are not connected to the rest of their lives. The physician never even spends an entire night with a woman, and he does not want a woman to live with him. But there is one consequence that cannot be evaded. If our actions are transitory, our own being becomes unbearably "light," because what we do has no effect on anything. In contrast to promiscuity, faithful love affirms the significance of the lovers. Their being has "weight" because their sexual actions are deeply connected to the rest of their lives. For example, faithful love between two people can enrich their lives as both not only receive but also give love and affection. The illness or death of the beloved causes immense pain and dislocation. Faithful love thus gives "weight" to our actions and significance to life.

The other view of our actions is that they are permanent. Kundera illustrates this with Friedrich Nietzsche's theory of eternal return. Nietzsche speculates that, given an infinite amount of time, everything that has occurred must recur sooner or later. Nothing can be got rid of. But if our actions have permanence in this way, they become a burden: indeed, our evil actions, as they accumulate, become an unbearable burden.

The view that our deeds are permanent is not necessarily dependent on Nietzsche's theory of eternal return. It may also rest on a commitment to justice. It would be unfair if the good and evil we do were not suitably rewarded and punished. Plato and Kant took justice so seriously that they postulated a final judgment after this life because all too often people's good actions are not properly rewarded and evil deeds are not properly punished. Both of them believed that no one should be able to escape the full consequences of the evil they have done simply by dying.

If good and evil are real, then what we do matters and our lives have significance. Unless there is forgiveness, however, we shall become so burdened by our evil that our lives become unbearable. Unless there is some way to remove our evil, we cannot be morally restored and we may even become crushed by its weight. But if good and evil do not exist, our deeds are transient and we become unbearably "light." We simply float, so to speak, because there is no moral order to which we belong.

If there is good and evil in the universe, there is a moral order. Our lives have a significance according to the degree to which they conform or fail to conform to it. Love and punishment are compatible in a universe in which our deeds matter, but in which our place is not determined solely by the moral value of our actions. In Christianity forgiveness is compatible with punishment because both of them have the same intention or purpose: to restore us when we depart from the way God intends us to live. God offers us forgiveness and his assurance that he will help us to live as we ought. He warns us that when we refuse to recognize his divine order, revealed in the Bible and at least dimly reflected in various moral systems, we shall be punished because our deeds have consequences. But many of us are troubled by an "unbearable lightness," because we deny the reality of good and evil and do not recognize the significance of our acts. Others of us are weighed down by a burden, which grows heavier and heavier as we accumulate evil deeds because we recognize the reality of good and evil, but not the forgiveness of God.

The man in the parable, who owed a debt that he could not pay, was punished because of his failure to be merciful. Even though the lord in the story was angry, the punishment was not vindictive. The man's heart was impervious to forgiveness, but punishment gets the attention even of the hard-hearted. The intention was to help him to learn that he ought to forgive others just as his lord had forgiven him.

Punishment is like medicine: it is intended to cure. We are warned that our deeds have consequences, that is, what we do matters. Out of love, we are offered release from all our debts and burdens. When we fail to receive God's forgiveness we shall suffer the consequences until we do receive forgiveness. God's will is that we suffer neither from the "unbearable lightness of being" nor from the unbearable burden of guilt. There is punishment precisely because what we are and do matters. The intention of God's punishment is that it should turn us to God so that we may receive his forgiveness, and not that our suffering should repay our debt.

God's mercy introduces a pause between our deeds and our receipt of the just consequence of our deeds. This pause may make it appear to some that they have evaded the consequences of their wrongdoing altogether, and even that right and wrong do not really matter. God's mercy, however, gives us the opportunity to be influenced by examples of decency and kindness, and by the threat that evil deeds eventually lead to dire consequences. Divine mercy is intended to lead people to repentance and the desire to follow his ways.

This is the attractive side of God's mercy. But it also has a side which seems less attractive to us. To introduce a pause between our deeds and their just consequence leads to innocent suffering. To temper justice with mercy means that for a time injustice is permitted. Believers, however, recognize that innocent suffering and unpunished wickedness do not mean that justice is mocked, but that they are inevitable in a universe in which there is mercy.

In a universe in which there is forgiveness, there are *breaks* in the normal sequences of causes and effects. For example, in teaching us to love our enemies and to pray for those who persecute us, Jesus instructed us to break the normal connection between injury and resentment. In this way we are children of God, belonging to God's *order*; for God's love is for everyone: those who obey him and those who do not. "He makes his sun rise on the evil and on the good, and sends rain on the just and the unjust" (Matt. 5:45). This too causes innocent suffering, because the love of enemies usually does not lead to reconciliation immediately, and sometimes there is no reconciliation. But it also gives a divine dimension to the actions of ordinary people.

Eric Auerbach in *Memesis* traces the origins of realism in western literature. In realist literary works, ordinary people's lives are taken seriously and what they do is significant. The story in which Peter denied that he knew Jesus in order to avoid arrest could not have occurred in the literature of ancient Greece and Rome because ordinary people's deeds were not considered a significant subject for serious literary treatment. Ordinary people in tragic situations were only suitable for comic treatment. Were the story of Peter's denial presented according to this canon, Peter would be portrayed as a buffoon, a figure of fun. In the Bible, however, a common person's betrayal of another because of fear is portrayed with reverence, as a temptation which every believer, whether socially important or not, may have to face. In *Memesis* Auerbach claimed that the form of literature we call realism, in contrast to classicism, developed because the Bible so saturated the outlook of western society.[4]

The scribes and Pharisees in Jesus' day did take the deeds of common people seriously. But they were as scandalized by Jesus' association with them as by his claim to forgive sins. What he taught was not in accordance with the law as they understood it; his claim to forgive sins was utterly unacceptable. Only God could forgive sins. Only the Holy One of Israel could break the connection between our deeds and their just desert. They were correct: only God can forgive sins. To claim to forgive sins, as Jesus did, was to claim to be God.

Three of Jesus' disciples witnessed a unique event that warranted this awesome truth, the transfiguration of Jesus. The significance of the event can be better appreciated through a comparison of the reactions of different people to Jesus just prior to its occurrence.

The fifteenth chapter of Matthew begins with a particularly sharp controversy between Jesus and the scribes and Pharisees. They charged Jesus with having taught his disciples to break the Jewish law. "Why do your disciples transgress the tradition of the elders? For they do not wash their hands when they eat" (Matt. 15:2). They were right: Jesus and his disciples did not wash in the ritually prescribed way. Jesus responded by accusing them of following a tradition that had perverted God's commandments. For example, they had circumvented the commandment, "Honor your father and your mother," through an ingenious interpretation that enabled them to avoid the cost of looking after their parents properly. "For the sake of your tradition, you have made void the law of God" (Matt. 15:6). He claimed that they were unable to interpret the law correctly because they had lost the spirit or intention of the law.

> Do you not see that whatever goes into the mouth passes into the stomach, and is evacuated? But what comes out of the mouth proceeds from the heart, and defiles

89

a man. For out of the heart come evil
thoughts, murder, adultery, fornication,
theft, false witness, slander. These are what
defile a man; but to eat with unwashed
hands does not defile a man (Matt. 15:17-
20).

But these scribes and Pharisees had too much invested
in their own tradition to be satisfied with Jesus'
explanation.

The next person Matthew mentions is a woman who
pleaded with Jesus to heal her daughter. She was a Canaanite, a descendent of the people from whom the Jews
had wrested control of Palestine. Although she was not a
Jew, she recognized that Jesus had the power to cast out
demons. Unlike the Jewish teachers of the law, she trusted
him. Jesus praised her faith, and healed her daughter.

Matthew then shows that ordinary people, in
contrast to the Jewish leaders, listened to Jesus' teachings.
Like the Canaanite woman, the ordinary people did not
understand who Jesus was, but they realized that his
teaching provided them with spiritual nourishment. In
their eagerness to hear him, a large crowd had followed
him for three days. They were short of food and hungry.
Out of compassion, Jesus fed them in a way that antici-
pated the Last Supper, that is, each person was given a
small piece of food. It gave them remarkable energy, so
that there was no danger of any of them fainting from
hunger as they returned home.

The sixteenth chapter of Matthew begins with the demand by the Pharisees and Sadducees that Jesus "show
them a sign from heaven" to authenticate himself. As far as
they were concerned, his power to heal people such as the
daughter of the Canaanite woman, and the greatness of

his teachings, which nourished the hearts of the common people, were not sufficient to establish that he was from God. Jesus told them that ample signs had already been given to satisfy those who knew how to read them. He would not provide a sign of the kind that would satisfy them, but told them that they would be given the Sign of Jonah. The allusion to Jonah was an allusion to his own resurrection from the dead.

In the Old Testament story, Jonah boarded a ship because he did not want to obey God's command to go to Nineveh, a non-Jewish city, where he was to proclaim God's judgment. Jonah realized that the storm which threatened to sink the ship was caused by his disobedience. To save the other passengers, he told the sailors to throw him overboard. Jonah was saved from drowning by being swallowed by a whale. After living in the belly of the whale for three days, he asked God to forgive him. The fish vomited him up safely onto a shore. This fable (and it was recognized as a fable in ancient times) was alluded to by Jesus as "the sign of Jonah." He too would be given up for dead, but would be raised by God's power to authenticate his claims. Jesus' remark to the Pharisees and Sadducees thus meant that they would have no other signs than the ones they had already been given, except for his resurrection from the dead. Jesus explicitly gave this interpretation to the phrase, "Sign of Jonah" in Matt. 12:38-41. It is of interest that Jonah and the whale was the first symbol used in art by Christians for their faith in Jesus.

The connection of his resurrection to the Sign of Jonah may account for Jesus' use of the word "leaven" in his warning to the disciples. "Take heed and beware of the leaven of the Pharisees and Sadducees" (Matt. 16:6). At first his disciples were confused because they had not brought any bread with them. Jesus reminded them of the food with which he had fed the crowd of people who had listened to his teachings. Then the disciples realized that he was warning them about the teaching of the Pharisees and Sadducees under the image of leaven, which is used to raise bread. Jesus had intimated to them that the teachings of the Pharisees and Sadducees could not raise people from the dead, but that his teaching could.

Matthew next describes the disciples reaction to Jesus when he asked them "Who do men say that the Son of man is?" (Matt. 16:13). The disciples replied, "Some say John the Baptist, others say Elijah, and others say Jeremiah or one of the prophets" (Matt. 16:14). In light of Jesus' controversies with the religious authorities, it was quite daring for people to think that he was a prophet. But it was conceivable, since prophets traditionally were at odds with the religious authorities of their own day. Unlike the authorities, many of the common people had been able to read the signs Jesus had given to the extent that they recognized that he was appointed by God, and that he ought not to be rejected. Jesus then asked his disciples, "'But who do you say that I am?' Simon Peter replied, 'You are the Christ, the Son of the living God'" (Matt. 16:16).

Jesus praised Peter warmly. But when Jesus explained that he must suffer and be killed, Peter was unable to take it in. He exclaimed "God forbid, Lord! This shall never happen to you" (Matt. 16:22). The promised Messiah was expected to establish justice and save Israel from unjust suffering. How could one who was rejected and killed do that? Even an uneducated fisherman knew enough theology to correct Jesus. Peter's blunder was echoed by those who stood at the foot of the cross and jeered, "He saved others; he cannot save himself" (Matt. 27:42).

Neither the Canaanite woman, ordinary people, nor the disciples had an adequate understanding of who Jesus was. What could Jesus do? How could he correct the disciples' misunderstanding and expand their minds to receive the truth? First, he forcefully rebuked Peter to make it clear that the common view about the Messiah, which Peter had uttered, was hopelessly perverted. "Get behind me, Satan! You are a hindrance to me; for you are not on the side of God, but of men" (Matt. 16:23). Peter was thinking as human beings think when they are under a foreign and rebellious influence, not under the influence of God's Spirit. Second, Jesus told them that after he had been rejected and killed, God would vindicate him, and that before their death they would see the Son of Man coming in his kingdom.

Immediately after this, Matthew describes the scene in which three of the disciples, Peter, James, and John, accompanied Jesus to a high mountain and witnessed Jesus' transfiguration.

> And he was transfigured before them, and his face shone like the sun, and his garments became white as light. And behold, there appeared to them Moses and Elijah, talking with him. And Peter said to Jesus, 'Lord, it is well that we are here; if you wish, I will make three booths here, one for you and one for Moses and one for Elijah.' He was still speaking, when lo, a bright cloud overshadowed them, and a voice from the cloud said, 'This is my beloved Son, with whom I am well pleased; listen to him.' When the disciples heard this, they fell on their faces, and were filled with awe. But Jesus came and touched them, saying, 'Rise, and have no fear.' And when they lifted up

> their eyes, they saw no one but Jesus only
> (Matt.17:2-8).

At the time of the Transfiguration the disciples could not comprehend its meaning. In Jewish piety, Moses represented the law and Elijah the prophets. Their conversation with Jesus suggests that they were in agreement and implied that Christ's teachings had, as he had claimed, fulfilled or completed theirs. In great fear, Peter blurted out that they would make three booths or tabernacles to honor Jesus, Moses, and Elijah. Peter recognized Jesus as equal to the greatest representatives of the Old Testament. But this is set aside by a voice that came from a cloud, "This is my beloved Son, with whom I am well pleased; listen to him" (Matt. 17:5). Jesus, as a beloved Son, is not only greater than Moses and Elijah, but in a class that transcends human greatness, and what he teaches is to be accepted. In awe, they fell to the ground.

John Calvin, the sixteenth century Protestant Reformer, claimed that what the disciples saw and heard was in a *vision*. This is supported by Matthew's comment that when Jesus reassured them by touching them and telling them not to be afraid, and they looked up, they could no longer see Moses and Elijah, and Jesus was no longer transfigured.

Calvin also noted, "Christ raises them up when they had fallen, and by so doing performs his office; for he came down to us for this very purpose, that by his guidance believers might boldly enter into the presence of God, and that his majesty, which otherwise would swallow up all flesh, might no longer fill them with terror. Nor is it only by his words that he comforts, but by *touching* also that he encourages them."[5]

These three disciples had a vision of Jesus in glory,

a preview of him in his resurrected magnificence. They were given the Sign of Jonah, Even though he would suffer and be killed, nonetheless he was the Messiah, and they would see him in the glory of the Resurrection. Although more transpired at Gethsemane and on the cross than they were able at the time to take in, they eventually realized that the cost of God's mercy was the death of his beloved Son.

John Calvin pointed out that the disciples' fear at the vision of Christ's glory was appropriate.

> If ungodly men mock at God, or despise him without concern, it is because God does not address them so as to cause his presence to be felt: but the majesty of God, as soon as we perceive him, must unavoidably cast us down.

Calvin's remark that some people can read the story of the Transfiguration without being affected by it because God has not cause his presence to be felt deserves careful consideration. The gospel writers do not ask us to be credulous: by their own admission the Transfiguration is far beyond our normal experience. Before we give credence to anything that is very unusual we require witnesses who can be questioned, and whose answers can be made available to others for scrutiny. But in the Gospel accounts all we are given is a story of a vision, and the story is not even given the same place in the sequence of events by different Gospel writers.

A popular way to deal with stories that stretch our minds because they contain a divine dimension is to classify them as myths. This enables scholars to examine such stories with academic seriousness, without having to accept or reject the tales as true. The stories can be carefully compared with the myths of other religions, and theories are devised about the significance of myths. This is a legitimate procedure, but the definition of the category of myth does not include an essential feature of the Gospel stories: they bear witness to the Incarnation.

In the Bible a witness is whoever or whatever God uses to cause his presence to be felt or his truth known. For example, it is not sufficient to have been present when Jesus healed someone to recognize God's truth. According to the Gospel stories, some people who were present when Jesus performed healings did not recognize that the power by which Jesus healed was from God; nor did they accept what Jesus was teaching about God through a particular healing. A witness to God always raises for people the issue of their own allegiance to God. Before a witness to God, the issue of whether God's presence or truth is to be accepted or rejected can be avoided only by a person's blindness, misunderstanding, or evasion.

A study of the Gospel stories *exclusively* under the category of myth is methodologically blind to these dimensions. There is no need to consider the possibility that God may use them to cause divine presence to be felt or truth to be known. It filters out the questions they pose about one's own allegiance by neither rejecting them nor accepting them.

Blaise Pascal, the seventeenth century mathematician and scientist, who also gave serious attention to religious matters, has some sound advice about the Bible. He wrote, "One must know when it is right to doubt, to affirm, to submit. Anyone who does otherwise does not understand the force of reason. . . ."[6]

Without trying to give an exposition of Pascal's deep remark, we may nonetheless accurately apply it to the matter at hand. By historical investigation, we have learned quite a lot about Jesus, for example, that he taught with authority and that his teaching led to controversy. But whether he had the authority *of God* to give definitive interpretations of the Jewish law, and to have the power to forgive sins are beyond the scope of historical investigation. Historical investigation establishes that he was crucified on account of what he did and taught, but whether his death redeems those who follow him from sins and evil is beyond historical methods. By means of our intellect(or common sense) we can see that historical investigation cannot be used to determine the verity of what is most important in the Gospel stories. But when we are beyond the boundaries of historical investigation we are not in the domain of the irrational or unreasonable. We are in the place in which God's presence can be felt and the truth known. It is a place in which each of us must take personal responsibility for how we respond.

1. Stern, Menachem. *Greek and Latin Authors on Jews and Judaism*. Jerusalem: Israel Academy of Science and Humanities, 1974; 1: 115, 149, 155, 216, and 2: 375.

2. Another aspect of this parable is treated in my book: *Love: Christian Romance, Marriage, and Friendship*. Cambridge, MA.: Cowley Publications, 1987.

3. Kundera, Milan. *The Unbearable Lightness of Being*. Michael H. Heim, trans., New York: Harper & Row, 1984. In Kundera's story, the physician finally does live with a woman, whose faithful love eventually enables him to escape from the "unbearable lightness of being."

4. Auerbach, Erich. *Memesis*. Willard R. Trash, trans., Princeton: Princeton University Press, 1953.

5. Calvin, John. *Commentary on the Harmony of the Evangelists*. Wm. Pringle, trans., vol. 2. Grand Rapids, MI.: Eerdmans, 1949.

6. Pascal, Blaise. Penseés, Fragment no. 170. A.J. Krailsheimer ed., trans., Baltimore: Penguin, 1980.

7. I examine this question more in my book: *Three Outsiders: Pascal, Kierkegaard, and Simone Weil*. Cambridge, MA.: Cowley Publications, 1983.

CHAPTER SIX

Pathways to God

An examination of the Gospels has shown that the way God's power and truth made themselves felt in various people's lives differed considerably. It was not the same for Mary Magdalene as it was for the centurion whose slave had a deathly illness; Peter, James, and John experienced God's presence in still a different manner. We shall now examine two non-biblical people's experience of the reality of God, and conclude with some remarks about how we may find God in our own lives.

I will begin with an examination of the path to conviction followed by two highly accomplished, well-educated, and critically minded people: Leo Tolstoy, considered by many to be the greatest novelist of the nineteenth century; and Simone Weil, a philosopher and political activist of the 1930s. Tolstoy's religious milieu was Russian Orthodoxy, Weil's was Roman Catholicism, but their accounts are relevant to people with different backgrounds.

Let us first examine Tolstoy's description of his recovery of commitment to the Christian faith, which he had discarded as a young man. For about a year Tolstoy says that his

> .... heart was oppressed by a tormenting
> feeling, which I cannot describe as other-
> wise than as a searching after God.[1]

In any search, we are looking for what we do not have. Tolstoy's search was motivated by "a tormenting feeling." Eric Remarkque, in his novel *Night Out of Lisbon*, ironically compared the way people often think that they are seeking God to people who say they want to learn how to swim, but who insist on remaining fully clothed—with hat, overcoat, gloves, and heavy shoes—holding a bulging suitcase in each hand, and with a knapsack on their backs. Just as we must set aside our clothing and other impediments in order to learn how to swim, so, too, we must set aside the idea that the things of this world can give us complete and lasting satisfaction in order to seek God. Our need for God, which causes us to feel dissatisfied with life, does not always reach the intensity of a tormenting feeling, as it did for Tolstoy, but without an awareness that something vital to life is missing, a search for God is not an authentic one.

Tolstoy continues:

> This search ... was not an act of my reason,
> but a feeling, and I say this advisedly,
> because it was opposed to my way of think-
> ing; it came from the heart. It was a feeling
> of dread, of orphanhood, of isolation amid
> things all apart from me, and of hope in a
> help I knew not from whom. Though I was

> well convinced of the impossibility of prov-
> ing the existence of God—Kant had shown
> me, and I had thoroughly grasped his rea-
> soning, that this did not admit of proof—I
> still sought to find a God, still hoped to do
> so, and still, from the force of former habits,
> addressed myself to one in prayer. Him
> whom I sought, however, I did not find.

We have already considered the feelings Tolstoy described. We said that the feeling of dread is the result of the
image of God. The life God intends us to have implies that
our present life, for all its goodness, is by itself inadequate
to satisfy us. Our awareness of its inadequacies fills us
with dread, especially when we consider the inevitability
of suffering, the loss of loved ones, and our own death. The
feeling of orphanhood is the result of not having yet found
a point of reference that would enable us to find our place
in the order. The sense of isolation is a result of the lack of
apparent purpose in natural processes and human activity.

Tolstoy's search for God was not an act of reason
because he had accepted Kant's refutations of the so-
called traditional proofs for God's existence. According to
Kant, it is a mistake to believe that the drive inherent in our
reason for complete knowledge has its proper termination
in God. Kant was intent to show that it was beyond the
power of our reason to produce arguments that establish
God's existence with a logic that is water-tight. Why did
this trouble Tolstoy? Most religious people are not troubled when they learn of Kant's refutations because their
belief in God is not based on the so-called traditional
proofs of God's existence, just as the belief of people in
biblical times was not based on them. Unlike them, how-

ever, Tolstoy had not yet found God, and he believed that the only way to establish the reality of God was by rational proofs. People who do not believe in God and who are not seeking God are also not troubled by Kant's refutations. Without an awareness of a need for God, they do not find themselves in a quandary, as did Tolstoy.

Tolstoy's previous religious training ("the force of former habits") enabled him to find a way to God, namely prayer. Apparently, he did not realize that he was actually following the path frequently recommended by spiritual guides, such as Teresa of Avila, as we saw earlier. Tolstoy found that his prayers, however, were not answered immediately.

> ... the more I prayed, the clearer it became that I was not heard, that there was no one to whom to pray. With despair in my heart that there was no God, I cried, "Lord, have mercy on me, and save! O Lord, my God, teach me!" But no one had mercy on me, and I felt that life stood still within me.

But Tolstoy's need for God, which included a sense that his life had significance and purpose, enabled him to continue to pray.

> Again and again, however, the conviction came back to me that I could not have appeared on earth without any motive or meaning ....

Persistence in prayer has a direct parallel in experimental science. Russell Stannard, who directed a research team that confirmed the existence of the fourth kind of quark, called "charm," used his experience in small-particle physics to answer a young woman's question about how to find God. Although he had estimated the odds of confirming the existence of charm by the experiments his team had prepared as about one out of five, they had not put less effort into their preparations than they would have done if the odds had been higher. One hundred percent effort, so to speak, had had to be made, even though the odds of success were less than twenty percent. He and his colleagues invested two years of their scientific lives to plan, prepare, and conduct experiments that might well fail. If it took concentrated effort for two years to confirm the possible existence of a sub-atomic particle, Stannard thought it reasonable to advise the young woman to set aside five minutes each day for two years for prayer. Not just prayer but *persistent* prayer is needed in our search for God.[2]

Tolstoy eventually found that his prayers had an effect.

> "He is," I said to myself. I had only to admit
> that for an instant to feel that life re-arose in
> me, to feel the possibility of existing and
> the joy of it.

The sheer affirmation of God deeply moved Tolstoy because he was so seriously engaged with the question of the reality of God. Often our words and prayers do not have this or comparable effects on us because our attention is not focused on God. We have violated the commandment, "You shall not take the name of the Lord your God in vain" (Exodus 19:7); that is, we have used God's name in such a way that it has had no effect on us.

The ineffectiveness of our words and prayers can be compared to the ineffectiveness of racing a car engine. All drivers know that, unless the gears are engaged by moving the gear lever, the car will not move, however much they push on the accelerator. The engine will simply whirl around faster. So, too, with our talking and praying. Unless we are seriously engaged, our words and thoughts are in vain. They do not move us, as did Tolstoy's words and prayers, from distress to joy.

Even though Tolstoy's words and prayers led to joy, this result was not of itself sufficient to give him a lasting conviction of the reality of God. He was led to question whether the effect of his affirmation of God and his prayers was psychologically induced by his own mental processes, rather than being caused by God.

> . . . My joy, though, did not last long, for reason continued its work: 'The conception of God is not God. Conception is what goes on within myself; the conception of God is an idea which I am able to rouse in my mind or not as I choose; it is not what I seek, something without which life could not be.' Then again all seemed to die around and within me, and again I wished to kill myself.

This doubt was overcome when he became clear in his own mind about what finding God means.

> After this I began to retrace the process which had gone on within myself, the hundred times repeated discouragement and revival. I remembered that I had lived only when I believed in a God. As it was before, so it was now; I had only to know

> God, and I lived; I had only to forget Him, not to believe in Him, and I died. What was this discouragement and revival? I do not live when I lose faith in the existence of a God; I should long ago have killed myself, if I had not had a dim hope of finding Him. I only really live when I feel and seek Him. "What more, then, do I seek?" A voice seemed to cry within me, "This is He, He without whom there is no life. To know God and to live are one. God is life."
>
> Live to seek God, and life will not be without Him. And stronger than ever rose up life within and around me, and the light that then shone never left me again.

To know God and to live are one because God is *zoe*, the uncreated life. With this realization, the cycle of misery and elation ceased, and "the light that then shone never left [him] again."

Since God seeks us, we do not need to rely on arguments that establish God's existence because knowledge of God is possible through conscious *interaction* with God. To experience the effects of the divine life in our own lives can lead to a firm belief in the reality of God. The reason religious faith is not credulity is because it is anchored in contact with the uncreated life of God (*zoe*), which is often referred to as grace or as the Holy Spirit. More than contact is needed to produce rational conviction, as we will see even more clearly in Simone Weil's account of her spiritual journey, but it is because divine grace is being received that people enter a path that leads to conviction.

Christianity cannot be reduced to mere feelings, however, because this would not include the fact that we must change the way we live. To interact with God is to recognize that our lives must be changed to become increasingly like God's life, as we saw in our study of Jesus' teachings. One way to recognize in our lives that what we feel is the result of interacting with God is that we find ourselves seeking to have our lives conform to his order.[3]

When Tolstoy came to an explicit faith in God, he simultaneously had the conviction that he should obey God's will.

> It was strange, but this feeling of the glow
> of life was no new sensation; it was old
> enough, for I had been led away from it in
> the earlier part of my life . . . . I returned to
> faith in that Will which brought me into
> being and which required something of
> me; I returned to the belief that the one
> single aim in life should be . . . . to live in
> accordance with that Will; . . . in other
> words, I returned to a belief in God . . . . .

The path we follow to achieve contact with God need not be precisely the same as the one Tolstoy followed. We have examined his carefully because it contains many features that are commonly found in the lives of people who have come to faith in God. Frequently there is a conscious need for God and a search for him. Often there are barriers to belief in God that put the seeker into a quandary. For Tolstoy, it was a belief that rational arguments for divine existence were the only path to God. For some people today, it is the notion that science has made belief in God implausible; for others, it is a concern about the trustworthiness of the Bible or a lack of confidence in the credibility of a Church's teachings. These difficulties are often mitigated or removed by a greater understanding of what Christianity teaches. Persistent prayer and participation in worship, on the one hand, and recurrent doubt, on the other, are commonly found in accounts of pilgrimages to a firm and settled faith. Finally, clarification is achieved about what finding God means. In general, there is a recognition that to receive spiritual nourishment from Christian teachings, worship, and practices is to be in contact with God. This recognition of God's reality includes a desire to live a life that is in accord with the divine will.

The next path to God that we shall examine is the one followed by Simone Weil. It shares some of the features we have just mentioned, but it is significantly different from Tolstoy's. Tolstoy was driven to seek God by a feeling of torment. Weil's initial experience of the reality of God was not the result of a conscious searching. She tells us that when reciting George Herbert's poem "Love," she had what in spiritual theology is called a divine visitation.

> Often at the culminating point of a violent headache, I make myself say it over, concentrating all my attention upon it and clinging with all my soul to the tenderness it enshrines. I used to think I was merely reciting it as a beautiful poem, but without my knowing it the recitation had the virtue of a prayer. It was during one of these recitations that, as I told you, Christ himself came down and took possession of me.

> In my arguments about the insolubility of the problem of God I had never foreseen the possibility of that, of a real contact,

person to person, here below, between a
human being and God.[4]

More than this visitation was needed to convince Weil
of the reality of God. ("I still half refused, not my love but
my intelligence"). Full conviction came only with repeated experiences of God's love, which she reports occurred when praying, and with the development of her
views on beauty.

In the context of a discussion of the evidential force of
Christ's miracles Weil writes,

> The exceptional character of the acts had
> no other object than to draw attention.
> Once the attention has been drawn, there
> can be no other form of proof than beauty,
> purity, perfection.

Weil points out that in the New Testament miraculous
acts are a sign that the person who performs them is
outside the ordinary run of humanity. He or she is the
servant either of supernatural good or of supernatural
evil. Weil claims that it is easy to see "by the manifest
perfection of Christ, the purity of his life, the perfect
beauty of his words, and the fact that he only exercised his
powers in order to perform acts of compassion" that Jesus
was allied to supernatural good. Accordingly, we are to
believe all that he said,

> save where we have the right to suppose a
> faulty transcription; and what gives the
> proof its force is beauty. When the subject
> in question is the [supernatural] good,
> beauty is a rigorous and positive proof;

and, indeed, there can be none other. It is
absolutely impossible for there to be any
other.

Why does beauty function as a rigorous proof of supernatural good? Weil argues that the entire order of the
physical universe operates as it does without any choice.
When nature's operations hurt us, the universe seems to
us to be *merely* a brute force. But,

> brute force is not sovereign in this world. It
> is by nature blind and indeterminate. What
> is sovereign in this world is determinat-
> eness, limit. Eternal Wisdom imprisons this
> universe in a network, a web of determina-
> tions. The universe accepts passively. The
> brute force of matter, which appears to us
> sovereign, is nothing else in reality but
> perfect obedience . . . . That is the truth
> which bites at our hearts every time we are
> penetrated by the beauty of the world. That
> is the truth which bursts forth in matchless
> accents of joy in the beautiful parts of the
> Old Testament . . . .[5]

Her reasoning seems to be that beauty is a property of
the order of the universe. The beauty of the universe is not
a property of brute force, because we love the beauty of the
universe and are repelled by brute force. The order of the
universe, since it has a property (beauty) that is not a
property of brute force, is not caused by brute force. The
beauty of the world is thus a sure sign or mark that the
order of the universe arises from a supernatural good. This
view of beauty led Weil to claim that "beauty is a rigorous

and positive proof" of divine activity.

More investigations of this kind, as well as more experiences of God's love in prayer, finally led Weil to full conviction of the reality of God. A single experience, even one as powerful as a visitation, was not sufficient. Nonetheless, that experience gave her the incentive to examine an enormous amount of material in philosophy and in various religions of the world and to develop her theory about beauty as a sure mark of supernatural truth.

Although both Tolstoy and Weil experienced contact with God, each needed more than experience to satisfy their minds. Tolstoy's reflections initially were centered on the cycle of misery and joy in his life, but he relied on Christian teachings to enable him to know what finding God means. Weil's reflections focused on the beauty of the world. But in both cases the result was the same: an explicit faith in the reality of God.

We do not have to accept either Tolstoy's or Weil's reasoning to see that their experiences initiated and motivated their efforts to bring heart and head together. They would not have made the effort were their hearts not deeply and profoundly moved. Each of them illustrates Plato's claim that we so passionately care about what is ultimately true because we have been moved by love.[6]

To come to faith in God, contact with God does not need to be as dramatic as Tolstoy's or as spectacular as Weil's. To be moved by Jesus' teachings and life is to have been touched by the love of God. Even a single incident in Jesus' life or one of his teachings may awaken a love that opens a path, which if pursued with persistence, leads to full conviction. Extraordinary experiences should therefore not cause us to overlook the unprepossessing way that the Gospel stories lead us to God.

The Gospel stories themselves may cause people to

have extraordinary experiences. People, who have had a dramatic conversion experience and describe themselves as "born again" Christians, sometimes assume that to be a full-fledged Christian, a person must have a conversion experience. People who consider themselves to be Christians, but who have not had a dramatic conversion experience, question this assumption. Those who are "born again" Christians are deeply hurt by this questioning.

If both parties agree that in Christianity the crucial thing is to be devoted to God, this friction can be avoided. The word "conversion" means "to turn toward." The redirection of a person's life may be very sudden, so that he or she is very much aware of the change, as was Tolstoy, or a person may change the direction of his or her life so gradually that there is no awareness of any dramatic change. A gradual change can result in a complete redirection. For example, if we raise an arm vertically, in twelve hours it will be pointed in the opposite direction because of the rotation of the earth. Even though the earth turns at the rate of a thousand miles per hour, we do not feel it. The main issue in Christianity is whether or not we are devoted to God, not whether we turned toward God *so rapidly* that we felt the change in the direction of our life, or turned so gradually that we did not feel the change.

To insist that a person must have a conversion experience puts the stress on the *experience of turning*, not on the *direction* of a person's life. Whether a commitment to the Christian life takes place suddenly or gradually, it is because of the Spirit of God which comes "from above" (John 3:3). There is room in Christ's kingdom for both those who have and those who have not had a conversion experience. I personally am glad that I had such an experience. It would be better were I as good a Christian as a friend of mine who has not had a conversion experience,

111

and who tells me that she cannot think of a time in her life in which her heart did not respond gladly to stories about Jesus.

My conversion experience happened during my last year of high school. At that time my life was going well: I was making good grades; I was well-liked at school; I had even been entrusted with looking after my father's small business when he took a much needed vacation. One evening I was discussing religion with two college students, one was a devout Roman Catholic and the other a staunch Southern Baptist. Although they were friends, they frequently argued about religion. Their wrangling made me wonder what God required of us. Although I had been regularly attending a church for three or four years, my understanding of Christianity had no focus. I certainly thought of myself as a decent person and a Christian. But the Southern Baptist told me that God expected perfection. To have disobeyed any commandment even once was enough to condemn a person to hell. But if we believed that Christ had died for us, God would mercifully pardon all sin freely. I was stunned. The life that pleased me so much was utterly, and hoplessly unacceptable to God. But I was also thrilled to learn that all I had to do was accept God's forgiveness.

For several weeks I was euphoric. But in time, the euphoria faded. I began to worry: did I really believe that Jesus was my savior? How could I tell whether I believed or not? I asked various born again Christians, but their answers did not help. One asked me if I had a secret sin (I didn't). Another pointed out that about eighty percent of the people who have a conversion experience later have a let down. To be told that I was one of the eighty percent did not tell me why there was a let-down or how to get out of it. I now realize that a common solution for people in my condition is to attend a revival meeting in order to rekindle the feelings experienced at the time of conversion. But revival meetings did not help me, because revivalists only repeated in different ways the theme that Jesus saves and that all we need to do is believe this, whereas my problem was that I did not know how I could tell whether I believed it or not.

Soon after this I began college. I was exposed to such rich and diverse ideas and experiences that the revivalist theology was not deep enough or broad enough to make sense of what I was learning. For me the revivalist teaching was rather like the one talent given to the man in Jesus' parable. The man was severely rebuked by his master, because he had buried the talent, rather than used it to increase the treasure entrusted to him. It was only by attending churches and associating with Christians, who taught me much more than one can get from a revival meeting, that I learned that a person does not need to have a particular feeling of being born again to be a follower of Christ. I am grateful to that revivalist college student, who told me I needed a savior, but my conversion experience by itself would never have been enough to hold my commitment. However much my heart was moved, my mind had to be satisfied.

As I have shown in this book, even though all of us are sinners, Christ did not approach everyone by telling them that they were sinners. He approached people in different ways. He did not say the same thing to them all, because each of them was different.

Now that we have examined several pathways to God, we shall examine a place where contact with God is particularly important to us as individuals and to society at large. According to Christ's teachings, we are to love our neighbors. Love is to motivate our actions. But do our motives make any difference to our society? Are they simply a matter of personal preference? Pascal, for example, points out that one person can do a task for money and another person can do the same sort of task out of love. The motivation is different, but the results may be very much the same. An organization or an entire society can be based on people's desire for personal gain and prestige, rather than on the Christian virtue of love.[7]

Consider, for example, the airline industry. The cooperation between mechanics, flight attendants, pilots, and flight controllers is remarkable. Their cooperation makes it possible for people to be transported efficiently and safely. But they would not work together were they not paid. An airline is run for money, not for love. As long as people cooperate, does it matter what their motives are?

The need and desire to be paid are not necessarily in conflict with higher motives, such as Christian love. As Pascal puts it, a tall person and a short person both stand on the ground. A person, who has no means of support, would not work without pay, but this does not mean that the only reason he or she does the work is for the pay. The question is whether having Christian motives makes a significant difference to the operation of an organization or to a society in general.

It is clear that conscientious people suffer because of their motives. Consider, for example, the field of education. It is a challenge to live up to the aims of education with personal integrity. It is all too easy for an institution to penalize actions which promote genuine education and to reward actions that do not. For example, many institutions reward publishing, but only pay lip service to good teaching and to the effort devoted to individual student needs. In such a situation, teachers, who care for genuine education, are caught in a bind. If they succumb to "the system," they feel guilty. If they do not succumb, they may become angry and grow bitter because they are not properly rewarded, while others, who go along with the system, are unjustly rewarded. For those who care about the goals of an organization, the issue of integrity is unavoidable because no organization's system of rewards and punishments matches perfectly the aims of the organization.

Even should an organization's pattern of rewards and punishments be basically in line with the aims of education, and so encourage positive educational results, the system of rewards and punishment itself cannot create *allegiance* to the aims. In one way or another the lack of allegiance to those aims will show in the results. An airline, which depends solely on pay and prestige as rewards and punishment, will not provide as good a service as one that also has people working for it who do more than they are paid to do, or do more than they are praised for doing. Likewise, a school or college that depends on pay and prestige *alone* will not achieve as much as a school or college with teachers and administrators who are motivated by the desire to educate people. The rewards of money and prestige can sometimes *approximate* but not yield precisely the same results.

In an organization or in a society that is in good working order, the social significance of people's motives is easily overlooked. The need to deal with the burden of guilt, anger, and bitterness that results from the struggle for personal integrity seems to be a private matter only. But if the burdens they bear are not alleviated, there will be progressively fewer and fewer people who will continue to try to achieve the aims of an organization or the goals of a society, such as providing decent housing and health care for all citizens. Unless *enough* people continue to operate from higher motives, organizations and society in general will suffer. When too many people are concerned with themselves only, so that we can appeal only to their lower motives, we find ourselves forced to spend, say, $60,000 a year to get the results we once were able to get for $20,000 a year. With a further decline in the number of committed people, it will take even more money to get the results that once were possible for $60,000. A society may find itself reaching a situation in which no matter how much money is spent, some of its earlier goals cannot be achieved because there simply are not enough of the right sort of people left in the society. This drift was an important factor in the decline of ancient Rome. It is perhaps beginning to happen in our own society in such fields as education, finance, law, and medicine.

Contact with God helps to relieve the burdens of guilt, anger, and bitterness that trouble conscientious people. But why does contact with God have this beneficial effect? Evil cannot remove evil. For example, if there is someone in a family or an organization who is jealous or envious, his or her resentment will usually provoke others and lead to other evils. Their resentment is mitigated only by those people who have sufficient goodness to overcome their natural reaction to respond to evil with evil. By refusing to respond to evil with evil, a good person can cause evil to vanish. If there is someone with enough goodness, any evil can be absorbed; if there is someone who is inexhaustibly good, all evil can be absorbed.

Only God is perfectly good, and never responds to evil with evil, and only God is inexhaustibly good. God's goodness is not remote. It is accessible to us through prayer and worship. It is accessible to us in the lives of people who are in contact with God. It is reflected in the beauty of the universe. God's goodness is not obtrusive.

We can easily avoid taking part in religious rites in which the incarnate Word of God, who endured evil without returning evil, is present. For example, sociologically churches are classified as "voluntary organizations," implying that membership is an option we may exercise, rather like an elective course, not part of the core curriculum of life. We can easily set aside the positive effects of good people by ignoring their example of not responding to evil with evil and by trying to take advantage of them. When our minds are fixed on personal gain and prestige, the beauty of the world is of no interest. Yet it is contact with God which inspires lives and relieves burdens, so that a society and its organizations have people in them who act as yeast that raises them to greater heights.

Our final word about finding God is one of caution. As we all know, algebra books often have answers printed in the back. Although the answers are correct, to know the answers does not mean we know how to work the problems. To know the Christian answers to the big questions of life does not mean that we know God. We cannot grasp God by just knowing the right words. As Jesus said, "The wind blows where it will, and you hear the sound of it, but you do not know whence it comes or whither it goes; so it is with everyone who is born of the Spirit" (John 3: 6-8). We only learn to have contact with God in our daily life with repeated effort, for we are dealing with a truth that is alive. E. M. Forster captured this nicely in his novel, *Howard's End*:

> The business man who assumes that this
> life is everything, and the mystic who as-
> serts that it is nothing, fail, on this side and
> on that, to hit the truth. 'Yes, I see, dear; it's
> about halfway between,' Aunt Juley had

hazarded in earlier years. 'No; truth, being alive, was not halfway between anything. It was only to be found by continuous excursions into either realm, and though proportion is the final secret, to espouse it at the outset is to insure sterility'.[8]

1. Tolstoy, Leo. *My Confession*. New York: Thomas Y. Crowell & Co., 1887: 103.

2. Stannard, Russell. *Science and the Renewal of Belief*. London: SCM Press, 1982. Stannard points out that some people, perhaps unknowingly well-prepared and receptive, may establish meaningful contact with God much sooner.

3. For a philosophic defense of the reasonableness of relying on contact with God and the reasons to believe that we are in contact with God, see my book: *The Reasonableness of Faith*. Washington D.C.: Corpus Books, 1968.

4. Weil, Simone. *Waiting For God*. Herbert's poem "Love," may be found in any edition of his collection of poems entitled, *The Temple*.

5. ———— *The Need For Roots*. New York: Harper & Row, 1971: 268-9; 298. I present here only one of Weil's views on beauty.

6. See Socrates' speeches in Plato's *Symposium* and *Phaedrus*.

7. Pascal, Blaise. *Penseés* : Fragments 106, 118.

8. Forster, E.M. *Howard's End*. New York: Vintage Books, 1961.